Page Turners

Mercy Killer

Andrew Watson

Series Editor: Rob Waring

Australia • Brazil • Japan • Korea • Mexico • Singapore • Spain • United Kingdom • United States

Page Turners Reading Library
Mercy Killer
Andrew Watson

Publisher: Andrew Robinson
Executive Editor: Sean Bermingham
Senior Development Editor: Derek Mackrell
Assistant Editors: Claire Tan, Sarah Tan
Story Editor: Julian Thomlinson
Series Development Editor: Sue Leather
Director of Global Marketing: Ian Martin
Content Project Manager: Tan Jin Hock
Print Buyer: Susan Spencer
Layout Design and Illustrations: Redbean Design Pte Ltd
Cover Illustration: Eric Foenander

Photo Credits:
104 sjlocke/iStockphoto, **106** stray_cat/iStockphoto, **108** (top) Hywit Dimyadi/Shutterstock, (bottom) FotografiaBasica/iStockphoto

ISBN-13: 978-1-4240-1794-2

ISBN-10: 1-4240-1794-7

Heinle
20 Channel Center Street
Boston, Massachusetts 02210
USA

Cengage Learning is a leading provider of customized learning solutions with office locations around the globe, including Singapore, the United Kingdom, Australia, Mexico, Brazil, and Japan. Locate your local office at:
international.cengage.com/region

Cengage Learning products are represented in Canada by Nelson Education, Ltd.

Visit Heinle online at **elt.heinle.com**

Visit our corporate website at **www.cengage.com**

Printed in the United States of America
1 2 3 4 5 6 7 – 14 13 12 11 10

Contents

Review

Background Reading

People in the story

Dr. Rick Jamieson
a psychiatrist in a clinic
in Boston

Dr. Ian Kramer
Rick's boss

Jessica (Jess) Blake
a young woman

Professor Charles Agnew
Rick's friend and medical
advisor for large
pharmaceutical companies

Victor Adams
boss of Tamsus,
a pharmaceutical company

Detective Scott Anderson
a Boston police officer

The story is set in Boston, in the USA.

Chapter 1

A storm coming

Large clouds were beginning to circle the mountains. The rain was coming, too. Will knew it was dangerous to climb alone, but he really needed to clear his mind. He knew that the fresh air of Adirondack Park would help him to think. It would help him to decide what to do about the terrible secret he had discovered at work.

Now, after thirty minutes, he was deep in the park. He arrived at an enormous wall of rock, that rose high above the trees, and he stopped. He placed one hand on it, then he looked up at it and smiled. This was the challenge he needed.

He noticed a narrow path that went up around the side of the rock. *That must go to the top,* he thought. *I'll leave my things here. If it does start to rain, they will stay dry. And I can easily collect them after the climb.*

Only five feet from the top, a narrow shelf went from left to right. It was covered with grass that was waving in the wind.

I'll stop there for a rest, he thought. Will found a hold and pulled himself onto the rock.

It obviously wasn't a popular climb. He had to go slowly and use his fingers to brush away the loose earth from the rock. The wind was getting stronger, and then it started to rain.

Maybe I should go back, he considered. It was more difficult than he thought.

But Will was closer to the top than to the bottom now. *I have to go on,* he realized. He pushed everything from his mind as he used his strength and skill to climb higher.

Soon there was only one difficult move between him and the grass on the shelf above him. From there, the top was very close. He put his left foot into a deep line in the rock and used his right hand to grip a hold above his head. Then he pulled his body up and threw his left hand over the top.

I can't find a hold! he thought. His fingers were slipping and he started to lose his grip. *The rock's too wet! I'm going to fall!* And then, just in time, his fingers closed on a strong hold. A few seconds later, he climbed safely onto the narrow shelf.

His arms were tired. As his breathing slowed, he looked back down to the bottom. Almost twenty feet below, sharp rocks covered the ground. They had broken off and fallen down hundreds of years before.

It's a wonderful view, he thought. The thick forest covered the mountains far into the distance, and all around him large walls of rock pointed toward the gray sky. *But I still have to decide what to do. And now I know I have no choice. I have to tell the police.* After so much worry, the decision was a relief, and Will stood up to finish the climb.

It was only a few more holds to the top. *Almost there!* he thought. He could see the edge of the grass above. With a smile, he reached out to pull himself up those last few feet.

Will's hands were only inches from the top. Suddenly, a thick branch swung over the edge of the rock. It hit him hard in the chest. For a moment his fingers held him safe, then the rock seemed to twist away from him. He fell silently backwards, his eyes wide with confusion and fear.

Will Sutton never saw the person who killed him.

Chapter 2

The Lendax drug trial

"The timing of this is terrible. It couldn't be any worse!" Ian Kramer's thin face was worried.

Rick Jamieson looked up at his boss from behind his desk. "Will is dead and you're only worried about the timing?" he asked angrily.

"I'm not talking about Will's death, of course," answered Kramer. "I'm talking about the timing for us here at the clinic. I'm very busy right now with the East Coast Psychiatry Society conference. It's the biggest meeting for psychiatrists in the country and it only happens once a year. I want it to go well. But now there are only two of us. Without Will's help, you and I are going to have a lot of extra work."

Rick knew how important the conference was to Kramer. But the thought of extra pressure made Rick's heart beat faster. He hid his shaking hands beneath the desk. It was hard to believe that his best friend was dead. He hadn't slept well since he had learned of Will's accident, and it was beginning to show.

Rick and Will had done everything together. They met at medical school in Boston and had both decided to study psychiatry. "We already know so much about the human body," Will had said. "But we have so much more to learn from the study of the mind." Rick had agreed, and they had worked together ever since. They had even started work at Kramer's clinic on the same day.

"While I'm busy with the conference, you'll have to look after all our patients," said Kramer. "We may have to send some of them to another clinic until I can find a doctor to replace Will."

Rick nodded slowly. He wasn't happy, but Kramer was the boss.

"I understand that this is difficult for you, Rick, but do what you can. Everything will be easier for us both after the conference. Tamsus has agreed to pay some of the costs. They're one of the biggest pharmaceutical companies in the world and one of our most important drug suppliers. So I have to make sure that everything is perfect for the conference."

Whatever you say, thought Rick. As long as his patients had access to the drugs they needed, he wasn't interested in where the drugs came from.

"Right," said Kramer. "Let's get started. I'll send you the password for Will's computer so you can look at his patient files. And I'll transfer the details of his drug trial to my computer. I'll have to finish the experiment myself. We won't get paid if we stop it early."

Drug trials of all types were very common in the clinic. Every new drug had to be tested, and the drug companies paid for help with the tests. That was why Kramer encouraged trials in his clinic. He liked the extra money. Will and Rick were always managing trials of one sort or another.

"Which trial are you talking about this time?" asked Rick.

"The new antidepressant from Tamsus," answered Kramer. He stepped toward the door. "It's called Lendax. They say that it's the latest answer to depression. It's going to make millions of dollars for the company. The drug has just been licensed to confirm that it's safe. So Tamsus is now going to release Lendax for sale at the conference."

"If the drug already has a license, why is the trial still going?" asked Rick.

"Because Tamsus wants to compare their drug to the other antidepressants available. They want to prove that Lendax is the best drug there is."

As the door closed behind Kramer, Rick began to understand. In the weeks before Will's death, the two friends had seen very little of each other.

Now it makes sense, thought Rick. *Will must have been busy with the Lendax trial. He must have been trying to finish it in time for the conference.*

Rick thought back to the last time he had tried to meet with his friend. It was the day before Will died. "Let's have a drink tomorrow evening after work," Will had suggested to Rick. And Rick had called him the next morning to confirm. But then Will had said that he was too busy and cancelled the meeting.

Rick remembered the many weekends they had spent climbing together. Rick loved the open space of Adirondack Park, especially since his car accident. Eighteen months before, a tired bus driver had turned in front of Rick's car. The two vehicles had crashed into each other. Rick was trapped inside his car. For two long hours, he'd suffered a lot of pain as he waited to be released. He had experienced panic attacks ever since, especially when he was in small spaces like cars and elevators. Now, every time before he went driving, he always took drugs called beta-blockers to prevent the attacks.

Now, at the thought of the extra work, Rick realized that he was breathing faster. He began to feel all the signs of a panic attack coming, which he felt whenever he was stressed. His heart was racing and he started to sweat. The walls of the room seemed to be growing smaller.

Keep calm! he told himself as the sweat ran down his face. He tried to think of the open air outside the clinic. *Breathe slowly!*

As quietly as possible, he removed a small bottle of beta-blockers from his pocket and quickly swallowed two of the pills. Then he turned to the computer screen and waited for his hands to stop shaking and his heart to calm down.

It was a busy morning. Rick used Will's computer password to view his friend's files. Then he began to see patients. At about twelve o'clock, he finally stopped to make some coffee. When he returned to his desk, there was an automatic message on the computer screen. It was a list of Will's patients, and it showed which ones needed more drugs. Rick looked at the list. The third name was Adrian Blake, and the name of his medicine was Lendax.

Kramer has all the trial details on his own computer now, thought Rick, *but does he know that Adrian Blake needs more Lendax?*

Rick checked the appointment schedule for the week. No one called Adrian had made an appointment. That meant that Adrian wasn't coming to collect any more of the drug. Rick knew that it was important that Adrian continued taking the Lendax. Otherwise, he might lose any benefit of the treatment.

He needs more Lendax, thought Rick.

The possible consequences for Adrian were very serious. A patient who suddenly stops taking antidepressants can experience dangerous changes in mood. The drug must be taken regularly, sometimes for weeks or months.

I should check that Kramer's going to give Adrian more Lendax, thought Rick.

He picked up the phone and called Kramer's office to ask him. There was no answer. Then Rick remembered that his boss had meetings all afternoon. Kramer was organizing the East Coast Psychiatry Society conference.

He must have left the clinic already. Rick sighed. *I'll have to call Adrian Blake myself.*

Rick looked on the computer for Adrian Blake's file. He was looking for a telephone number so that he could arrange to give Adrian some more Lendax. He was surprised to see that, although there was a phone number and the information that Adrian was 26 years old, there was nothing about the Lendax trial in Adrian's file.

Kramer must have transferred all the other trial details to his own computer already, he thought.

Rick called the number, but there was no answer. Rick looked again at the computer and saw the patient's address: Adrian Blake lived on Charles Street, Beacon Hill. It was an expensive part of the city, just across the park from the clinic.

Rick looked at his watch. It was time for lunch, anyway. Maybe he could take Adrian some more of the drug himself?

Will's office was next door. Rick felt uncomfortable going into the room, but the trial drugs would be in the medicine cupboard in the corner. It was locked, but Rick had a key. Soon, he found a box with the name Lendax on the side. He opened it and looked inside.

Most antidepressants are pills, but Lendax was different. Rick was looking at a box of syringes. He read the words on the side of the box: "The property of Tamsus Plc. 28 Lendax anti-depressant syringes. Take one syringe each day. Empty the syringe directly into your arm or your leg."

Twenty-eight syringes, thought Rick. That would be enough for only four weeks. *I'll have to contact Tamsus to ask them for more. I'll complete the documentation after lunch,* he said to himself.

Rick put the box under his arm and began to walk toward Adrian's home.

The property of Tamsus Plc. 28
Lendax anti-depressant syringes.
Take one syringe each day.
Empty the syringe directly into
your arm or your leg.

The sidewalks were full of men and women. They were all hurrying between stores and offices. Their hands were full of paper bags, files, and briefcases. Every seat in the park was occupied. Everyone was enjoying the first days of spring.

Rick walked up Charles Street until he arrived at Adrian's house. Instead of a row of buttons to indicate an apartment block, Rick saw only one button. That meant that the whole house belonged to Adrian.

Will's patient must be a wealthy young man, thought Rick. He pressed the button and waited.

There was no answer. A light was shining on the second floor, so he tried ringing again. Then he reached for the large metal handle. At his touch, the door opened slowly.

If the door's not locked, then Adrian must be in, thought Rick. Inside, he could see the floor of a large hall. A big mirror on the wall reflected the darkness.

"Hello?" he shouted. "Mister Blake?"

The house was silent. Some stairs disappeared up into the shadows.

"Adrian?" Rick tried again. "It's Doctor Jamieson. I'm a friend of Doctor Sutton."

Again, there was no answer. Rick looked behind him once more and then nervously stepped inside.

His eyes slowly adjusted to the dark. A small oil painting was hanging opposite the mirror and some house keys lay on a table. He wanted to leave the box of Lendax and go. But the keys convinced him that Adrian was in.

Something is wrong, thought Rick. *If the door was open, the keys were there, and the lights were on upstairs, why was he not answering?* Rick climbed toward the light on the second floor.

The door to the front room was half open. Worried about what he might find, Rick pushed it and stepped through into a bedroom. Clothes and books lay all over the floor, and the sheets on the bed suggested many sleepless nights. Rick froze in shock. Adrian's body lay on the bed, motionless, his face a mixture of anger and sadness.

In the silence, Rick could hear his own heart beating fast. As he stepped forward, he noticed several empty syringes lying on the bed beside Adrian's body. On the side of each syringe, Rick could clearly read a single word, "Lendax."

Rick felt to see if Adrian's heart was still beating, but the body was already cold. When a noise came from behind, he turned. But before Rick could see anything, he felt a hard blow on the side of the head. As he fell across Adrian's body, Rick's mind faded into darkness.

Chapter 3

Rough treatment

Rick awoke and felt the carpet against his face. His head was hurting very badly. Slowly, painfully, he opened his eyes. When he saw the books and clothes beside him, he knew he was on the floor in Adrian's bedroom. He carefully raised himself onto his hands and knees.

"Don't move!" It was a woman's voice, cold and angry. "If you make one more move, I'll hit you so hard that you'll never move again."

Rick fought the pain in his head and tried to understand what was happening. "I'm a doctor," he said. "My name is Rick Jamieson. I'm Adrian's doctor. Please. Let me try to sit up."

"I said don't move!" repeated the voice. A foot pushed him back to the ground. "I'll hit you with this lamp again if you move one little bit." Rick recognized an emotion in the voice. It was something more than anger.

"Who are you?" he asked. "Are you a friend of Adrian's?"

This time the emotion was clear. The woman's voice was shaking as she answered, "I'm his sister."

Slowly, Rick turned his head. The woman was standing only a few feet away. She was still holding the big metal lamp she had used to hit him. She held it high in the air, ready to swing at him again. Her hair was dark and hung down to below her shoulders. She looked ready to react if he moved at all.

"What's your name?" he asked.

"If you're Adrian's doctor, you tell me," she replied.

"Uhh . . ." Rick was feeling faint and his heart was racing. It felt like the start of a panic attack. "Blake," he remembered. He struggled to stay calm. "Your name is Blake."

"You're a psychiatrist?"

"That's right. I came to check on Adrian. I found him like this."

The woman seemed to relax slightly, but she still held the light in her arms. "If you're a doctor, why would I take NSAIDs?" She was obviously testing Rick.

"NSAIDs are a type of drug that help with pain so . . . you'd take it for muscle pain, that sort of thing. Honestly, I am who I say I am."

There was a silence as the woman lowered the light she was holding. "He's dead, isn't he?" she asked.

Rick nodded. "I'm sorry." She quickly turned away to hide her tears. Rick stood silently. He didn't know what to say.

At last she turned back to him and wiped her eyes with the back of her hand. "I don't understand," she said. Her voice was hard again. She seemed determined to be strong. "I spoke to him just yesterday. He was fine . . . He . . ." The tears started again.

At last she put the light down and she shook her head. "It doesn't make any sense," she cried. "I haven't seen him in months. I've been working in Paris. But I speak to him all the time on the phone. And he never seemed . . ."

Rick understood her pain. But he knew that there was nothing he could say to help.

"Adrian was getting better," she started again. "He was going out and making new friends. He seemed to be enjoying life again." She looked down at her brother's body. Again, despite all her self-control, she continued to cry. She looked at Rick, and her blue eyes were full of sadness. "I wanted to surprise him," she said.

"You can't blame yourself. It's often impossible to tell if someone is going to do something like this."

The woman shook her head angrily. "I don't blame myself, Doctor," she said. "I blame you. You should have helped him." She pointed at Adrian's body. "He's your patient. And he's dead."

In the silence that followed, a low voice called from downstairs. "Hello?"

Detective Scott Anderson was a large man with sharp eyes and a face that always looked angry. It was as though he had forgotten how to smile. He nodded slowly as he questioned the woman quietly in the corner of the room. Two uniformed policemen stood by the door.

Rick's heart was still racing. His head hurt badly. As the woman answered each question, she stared angrily in his direction. Rick turned away, uncomfortable. He quietly removed the bottle of beta-blockers from his pocket and swallowed a couple of pills.

"Doctor?"

Detective Anderson was standing beside him. The woman had gone.

"I understand you're this man's doctor?"

"I suppose I am, yes."

"You suppose?"

"Well," Rick began to explain, but the thought of his friend Will's death was too much. So he didn't explain, he just nodded. "Yes, I'm his doctor. Rick Jamieson."

"So why did you come here today?" the detective asked.

"Adrian was about to finish his supply of drugs. I was bringing him some more."

"And what can you tell me about this?" Detective Anderson pointed at the syringes lying on the bed.

"That's the drug that Adrian was taking," answered Rick. "It's a new antidepressant called Lendax. Adrian was involved in a trial."

"So what's gone wrong?"

"It looks like Adrian took too much of the drug. And that probably caused a heart attack."

The detective turned to face Rick. "A heart attack?"

"It's a common problem with drugs like Lendax. Sometimes they can affect the heart. These drugs can be very effective against depression. But they can be dangerous if the patient takes too much."

"OK," the detective waved a hand. He had heard enough. "I'll need a statement from you later. If you give me your details now, I can let you go. We'll sort this out quickly. It looks like he killed himself—another suicide."

The next day, as Rick arrived for work he heard a voice that he recognized.

"Doctor Jamieson?"

He turned from the clinic door and saw Adrian Blake's sister. She was standing in the street. Her long brown hair was tied back and she looked very tired.

"I'm Jessica Blake," she said. "We met yesterday."

In Rick's mind, he could see again the tears on her face. "As I said yesterday, Miss Blake, I'm very sorry about your brother. But there's nothing more I can do for you."

"Please, call me Jess. And you're right. That's why I'm here. I've been waiting to see you. I want to tell you that I'm sorry about yesterday." Then she saw the mark from the lamp on Rick's face. "And sorry about hitting you. I didn't . . ."

Rick sighed. "That's OK, Jess. I understand. You don't need to apologize."

"There's something else, Doctor. I need your help. I need you to stop the Lendax trial. It's not safe."

Rick felt uncomfortable. He understood what Jess was thinking; she had lost her brother and now she wanted someone to blame. She had decided that it wasn't Rick's fault and so now she wanted to blame the drugs instead. But Rick knew that it wasn't so simple.

"Adrian was using Lendax as part of a trial, that's true," he said. "But the drug has already been licensed. That means that it's safe. The drug isn't responsible for your brother's death. I know that it's difficult to accept. But Adrian was a very unhappy man."

"He was getting better, Doctor Jamieson." Again, her voice was hard. "He was more positive. The Lendax must have upset his mind. You have to stop people using the drug. Otherwise it might kill someone else."

"I'm sorry, Jess, but we know that Lendax is safe. And I'm confident that Adrian had the best possible treatment we could give him." Rick turned back to the door of the clinic.

"Please listen to me. Adrian was getting better," Jess insisted. "I spoke to him on the telephone regularly, and I know that he was getting better. Only Lendax could have changed him so quickly. If you don't stop the trial, other patients will be in danger."

"Look, I told you," repeated Rick. "The drug has already been tested. In fact, the official release is in the next few days. I'm sorry, Miss Blake, but I have work to do."

As Rick watched her leave, he shook his head in sympathy and stepped into the clinic. Adrian Blake had suffered from depression, he reasoned. Rick wasn't surprised that he had killed himself. But it was sad, of course, and Rick felt sorry for Jess.

He had just gotten to his desk when the phone rang. He imagined it was Jess calling him from her cell phone. She was obviously a determined woman. He almost wanted to speak to her again. He wanted to try to explain again why he couldn't help her. But the voice was a man's.

"It's Detective Anderson here, Doctor. We met yesterday at the Blake home on Charles Street."

"Of course, Detective. Do you want that statement now?"

"That can wait, Doctor. This isn't about Adrian Blake. It's about someone called Miss Anna Richards."

"I'm sorry. I don't know that name."

"Would you check the clinic records, please?"

Rick was puzzled. He typed the name into his computer. In seconds, he was looking at a medical file for Anna Richards, aged 19, of Chelsea, Boston.

"OK, I've got her records in front of me," he said. "She's a patient of another doctor here, Will Sutton."

"Can I speak to Doctor Sutton?"

"I'm sorry," Rick said. The words felt trapped in his throat.

"Will was killed just last week. A climbing accident."

"I'm sorry to hear that, Doctor. Very sorry."

Rick could hear his voice shaking. "Adrian Blake was Will's patient, too. But what's all this about, Detective? Has Anna Richards done something wrong? I can't give you her medical files without a good reason."

"I don't think you need to hurry to do that, Doctor Jamieson. You see, she has just thrown herself out of her third floor window. And I noticed that she had a box of Lendax beside her bed."

Chapter 4

A dangerous drug?

As he put down the phone, Rick's heart was beating fast and he was sweating. He felt sick with anxiety. He reached again for the beta-blockers in his pocket.

Beta-blockers can be bought at most drug stores, but not without the permission of a doctor—they need a prescription. When he first started to need the pills, Rick should have seen another doctor to ask for a prescription. Instead, he had written a prescription for himself.

I can't let anyone know about the beta-blockers, Rick had thought at the time. *If I sign the prescription myself, I can keep it a secret.*

Rick was embarrassed that he had to rely on the pills. He was especially worried that Kramer would find out. His boss might think that Rick wasn't fit to work. Not even his best friend Will had known about the beta-blockers.

Now, in addition to the stress of all his extra work, two of the clinic's Lendax trial patients had committed suicide. Rick sat in a cold sweat as he waited for the pills to work. With each second, the beta-blockers slowed his heart. As he began to feel calmer, he tried to understand what was happening.

Two Lendax patients had killed themselves. First, Adrian Blake had given himself enough of the drug to end his life. Then a girl, Anna Richards, had thrown herself out of a window. But Lendax was supposed to balance their moods. The drug was meant to be helping them!

Rick remembered Jess's words: "If you don't stop the trial, other patients will be in danger." Was she right? Perhaps the drug wasn't safe. Maybe it affected a patient's mood in the wrong way? Maybe it gave the patients just enough energy to kill themselves?

But the drug has already been licensed, Rick thought. *The government has spent a lot of money checking it. They've said it's safe. If it wasn't, they wouldn't let it go on sale in just a few days!*

There was only one way to see if the deaths were unusual: he had to find out how many patients were involved in the trial. If it was a big trial with hundreds, or even thousands of patients, then two deaths wouldn't be significant. But if there were only a few patients trying Lendax, then two deaths was a large number.

I need to see the details of the trial, thought Rick. *But Kramer has removed all the details from Will's computer. I'll have to ask him directly. After all, he is managing the trial now. This is his problem.*

Rick tried to call Kramer in his office, but there was no answer. Then Rick remembered that Kramer was meeting that morning with the people from Tamsus.

He called Kramer's cell phone. "Ian," he said. "It's Rick."

"What is it, Rick? I'm very busy."

"The police have just called me. One of Will's patients, a nineteen-year-old girl called Anna Richards, has jumped out of her window. She's dead."

There was silence at the other end of the line.

"Ian?"

His boss sighed. "Yes, Rick, I'm here. And I'm sorry to hear that. But what can I do about it? I'm in the middle of a meeting with Tamsus."

"Anna Richards was part of the Lendax trial. So was Adrian Blake, the person I found dead yesterday afternoon."

"So two depressed patients have killed themselves. That's not unusual."

"But two patients from the same trial of the same drug?"

"What are you saying?"

"Maybe the Lendax isn't working."

"Rick," answered Kramer, "two patients have killed themselves. How do you know that's because of the drug? You don't know the size of the trial."

"Exactly," agreed Rick. "That's why I'm calling you. You've got all the trial details."

There was a pause as Kramer thought. "Listen," he began, "we've both got enough to do at the moment. We haven't time to worry about the Lendax trial now. I've seen the trial details; you haven't. The trial isn't testing Lendax's safety. No one is worried about that. The drug has already been licensed."

"Maybe we should be worried. Two of the patients in the trial have died. Maybe we should tell the others. They have a right to know. They might want to stop taking Lendax. Maybe we should offer them other antidepressants instead. It's not our decision."

"You're right, Rick," answered Kramer angrily. "It's not our decision. It's a decision for Tamsus. Our job is to supply them with patients and to report on the results. That's what we're paid for. And I'm not going to give you the details of the patients. If you contact them, you'll only worry them for no reason."

Kramer stopped and sighed. "Look, Rick, I'm sorry. I know that finding that body yesterday wasn't easy for you, but think about this. Two depressed people have committed suicide. That's a shame, but it's not unusual."

"So you're not going to do anything about it?"

"I'll report back to Tamsus as usual. They can decide if the deaths are significant."

"But that might be too late for the other patients!"

"Rick, I'm really very busy. The conference starts in two days. Lendax has already been licensed by the government. So I'm not going to question that decision. And I'm certainly not going to tell a major pharmaceutical company that their drug is dangerous when the government has already said that it's safe!"

"But . . ."

"We buy most of our drugs from companies like Tamsus!" Kramer went on. "This is not the time to upset them, particularly so close to the conference."

"But don't you think . . . ?"

"Rick!" interrupted Kramer. "I don't have time to argue. If there's a problem with the drug, Tamsus will find it when they review the trial results. This is their business, not yours. You have enough to do. I suggest that you get back to work. Good-bye."

Rick sat at his desk. He was angrier than ever before. Kramer seemed to care more for his business than for his patients! His boss was thinking only about money. Kramer didn't want to tell the other Lendax patients about a possible problem with the drug; otherwise those patients might pull out of the trial. And then Tamsus would stop paying Kramer. And they wouldn't sell their drugs to Kramer for such a good price.

I have to warn the other patients, Rick thought, *whatever Kramer says. If they're in any danger, I have to tell them. But I don't know who is involved with the trial. All the details are on Kramer's computer and I don't have the password. But maybe there's another way.*

He picked up the phone, checked a number on the computer, and called. Finally, a tired female voice answered.

"Hello?" the voice said.

"Jess, it's Doctor Jamieson here. I'm glad I got you."

"You were lucky," said Jess. It sounded as though she'd been crying. "I'm not staying here. This house belonged to my parents and I grew up here. But it's not the same now. I'm staying in a hotel. I'm just packing up Adrian's things."

"Jess, I need your help. Another Lendax patient has committed suicide."

"Now do you believe me?" asked Jess. "I told you that the drug isn't safe!"

"I'm starting to agree with you. Now I want to investigate the other patients in the trial. I need to ask you some questions."

"OK," she said.

"Did Adrian ever mention to you the size of the trial?"

"No. He just said that he was going to try a new drug. He had tried everything else. He said it was a drug that wasn't yet on the market. That's all I know."

"His doctor, Will Sutton, used to run support groups. Did Adrian ever mention going to one of those?"

"I don't think so. Why?"

"I need to find out who else was involved in the trial. My boss has a list of the other Lendax patients, but he's not going to help."

"Why not?"

"Because he's busy organizing a big conference. And he thinks the drug's safe because it's already been licensed. He may be right, but I think it's worth investigating."

Suddenly, Rick had an idea. The conference! His old teacher and friend, Professor Charles Agnew, was going to be at the conference. The professor was going to be honored with a prize for all his good work. Agnew was over sixty years old and was going to retire from psychiatry soon. Although he still worked with patients, Agnew's main job was to advise pharmaceutical companies. And one of those companies was Tamsus, the people who made Lendax! Agnew would be able to help.

"Jess," he said, "are you free this evening? There's someone I'd like you to meet."

Chapter 5

A serious threat

"Miss Blake, I was very sorry to hear about your brother."

"Thank you, Professor."

Professor Agnew looked at Jess with kind eyes. The man looked very distinguished yet young for his age. Jess found him very comforting. As he talked to her, the noise of the bar around them seemed to disappear. "It's always sad to lose someone we love," he said softly. "But to lose them after such a hard fight is particularly difficult."

Jess nodded. She was grateful for the professor's sympathy, but it made her want to cry again.

Rick saw that she was uncomfortable. He quickly spoke. "Professor," he said, "you've always helped me in the past. And I need your advice now."

Agnew turned to his old friend. "Of course, Rick. What can I do?"

"You still work for Tamsus, don't you?"

"That's right. In the last few years, I've been a medical advisor for many of the large pharmaceutical companies. I started working at Tamsus three years ago."

"And you know about their new antidepressant Lendax?"

"Of course," nodded Agnew. "I've not been involved with the drug myself, but everyone at Tamsus knows about it. There's a lot of pressure on it to do well. Victor Adams is the boss at Tamsus and he's spent millions of dollars on

research. So far, despite all that money, he has achieved very little. Everyone is hoping that Lendax will make a lot of money for Tamsus."

"Then I'm sorry to say that I've some bad news. Jess's brother Adrian was involved in a Lendax trial at our clinic. He's one of two Lendax patients who have committed suicide in the last twenty-four hours."

"I see," nodded Agnew. His face was very serious. "But you do understand, don't you, that Lendax has already been licensed? It has passed a series of strict tests, just like any other new drug."

"I understand that, Professor," said Rick. "But there are other drugs that pass but still show problems later. And it looks as if we might have a problem now. I'd like to make sure that Tamsus knows about the deaths. And if they can give me more details of the trial, I can warn the other patients as well."

Agnew looked at Jess and nodded slowly. Then he turned back to Rick. "If there is any reason to worry about Lendax," he said, "then, of course, those patients must be told. Why don't I arrange for you to meet the boss, Victor Adams? I'm sure I could get you a few minutes of his time."

"Thank you," said Rick.

"I warn you, though," Agnew went on, "Adams is very difficult to persuade. But if there's a problem, it's his responsibility to listen."

Rick turned with a smile to Jess. "You're very kind, Professor," she said. She shook Agnew's hand.

"Please don't mention it," said Professor Agnew. He stood up and smiled at them both. "I'll sort out this meeting and then call you tomorrow morning. And Rick?"

"Yes, Professor?"

"I haven't yet told you how sorry I am about Will. I was on holiday in California when he died, but I thought of you at the time. Will was a good man, and I know he was a good friend of yours. You and I have been friends since I taught you at medical school, Rick. If you ever want to talk about it . . ."

Rick's heart started to beat faster. He forced himself to smile. "Thank you, Professor. I appreciate that."

"Until tomorrow then," nodded Agnew. The professor smoothed his hair into place and then walked out of the bar.

Professor Agnew's influence was enormous. He arranged a four o'clock appointment for Rick and Jess with Victor Adams. Rick had to leave work early. He left the clinic quietly so Kramer wouldn't notice.

Tamsus was based outside of Boston. Before he collected Jess from her hotel, Rick had secretly taken a few beta-blockers. The pills helped him to stay calm for their brief journey in Rick's jeep.

Twenty-five minutes later, they arrived at a huge security gate. Behind it, a long drive led to the offices of Tamsus.

Rick parked his jeep in the shadow of the enormous office building, and stepped out, relieved to escape the enclosed space of the vehicle. The building looked like a large, dark box of glass. A receptionist took them from the front desk to the elevators, and Rick felt the beginning of another panic attack.

"What floor is Mister Adams's office on, please?" asked Rick. He was looking at the big elevator doors.

"Mister Adams is at the top of the building," answered the receptionist. "On the fourth floor."

"I think I'll walk up, then," answered Rick, trying not to sound nervous about being in an elevator.

Jess looked at him as though he were mad. "But that'll take you too long! Why do you want to take the stairs?"

Rick managed to smile casually. "I sit at a desk all day. I'd like a little exercise," he said.

"If you want," answered Jess. She stepped into the elevator. "See you up there!"

Happy to have escaped the elevator, Rick started up the stairs. A few minutes later, he arrived on the fourth floor. Jess was already waiting. Just then, the door opened and an enormous man appeared. His body was all muscle beneath an expensive suit. He waved them inside without smiling. "Doctor," he said. "Miss Blake. Come in."

As Rick and Jess stepped into the office, the enormous man walked toward the window. He stood there silently while Rick looked around. The room was huge. The walls were covered with expensive works of art. A small man sat behind a very big desk. His eyes stared at them through thick glasses.

"Welcome to Tamsus," said the little man. "I'm Victor Adams." He pointed to a couple of chairs opposite his desk. "Doctor Jamieson, I understand Professor Agnew is an old friend of yours?"

"That's right, Mister Adams," replied Rick. He sat down beside Jess. "The professor taught me at medical school."

Adams nodded. "He's a very intelligent man," he said. "He has helped us a lot." He turned to Jess. "And you, Miss Blake. Do you work in the medical world also?"

"A little," she answered. "I'm not a doctor, but I work for World United in Paris. We raise money for poor people around the world. It helps them to buy medical supplies and other things."

"I know World United," said Adams. "I admire the company very much. And yet I understand that it makes no profit?"

"All our profit goes back into the company," nodded Jess. "That allows us to help as many people as possible."

"I wish I could do the same," Adams said. "Unfortunately, I find that money is the best way to inspire the people who work for me. Anyway," he turned to Rick, "what can I do for you?"

"Mister Adams," answered Rick. "We're interested in the Lendax trial at our clinic. Unfortunately, two of our Lendax patients have committed suicide recently. One of those was Miss Blake's brother."

"Yes, I heard. I'm very sorry to hear that, Miss Blake. Very sorry indeed."

"That proves, doesn't it," answered Jess, "that Lendax isn't safe?"

Adams ignored her. He sat back in his leather chair and smiled at Rick. "Doctor, you say that these are your patients who have died?"

"Another of the doctors at my clinic, Will Sutton, was looking after them. He was responsible for the trial. Unfortunately, he . . . he died recently in an accident. Now I'm trying to find the details of the patients involved. I don't even know if they have enough of the drug to continue. It's your trial, so I was hoping that you can tell me."

Adams smiled again. "I'm sure you know, Doctor, that Tamsus is contributing toward this year's East Coast Psychiatry Society conference. I had a meeting yesterday

about the conference with your boss, Ian Kramer. He told me then about the deaths. He also told me that he is now going to continue the trial himself. He confirmed that it would be completed as agreed. So you really needn't worry. He and I will make sure that all the patients have enough Lendax."

"Mister Adams," answered Rick. His voice was growing louder. "It's your duty to warn the other patients in the trial about these two deaths."

Adams's eyes grew smaller. "You want to warn them to stop taking the drug?"

"Exactly!" shouted Rick. "They may be in danger. We have to tell them. And we have to stop the trial until we're sure that the drug is safe."

For several seconds, Adams stared at Rick. Then he turned to the big man by the window. "Patrick," he said, "you can go."

With a silent nod, the enormous man left the room. Adams turned back to his guests. "Doctor Jamieson, Miss Blake," he began. "We at Tamsus have been working on Lendax for nine years. That's nine years of development and tests. We are releasing the drug at the conference because we know it's safe. If we delay now, it will cost us millions of dollars. And millions of patients around the world who are waiting for this drug will suffer. You are suggesting that Lendax is not safe because two patients have killed themselves. But I'm not going to stop the release because a couple of depressed patients have committed suicide. I'm sorry that I have to be so direct," he looked at Jess, "but depressed patients do kill themselves sometimes."

"Then we have no choice," answered Rick. He stood up. "We'll contact the government and tell them about the deaths."

Adams laughed. "The government has already given us a license to sell Lendax! But if you speak to them, please say hello from me. I play golf with the state official most weekends. Now I'm afraid that I must get back to work. My receptionist will show you out."

Rick was shaking with anger. Adams had dismissed their worries so easily! As he turned the jeep back onto the main road, Rick wished that he had taken some more beta-blockers.

"What now?" asked Jess. "Can Professor Agnew help at all?"

Rick shook his head. "Not anymore. If the people at Tamsus think that he's making trouble, the professor's job will be at risk. Anyway, Agnew will be too busy now with the conference tomorrow."

"Is that the conference that Adams mentioned?"

"Yes. The East Coast Psychiatry Society." Rick pulled quickly into the busy fast lane. "Every year psychiatrists from around the country meet at a conference. They discuss new drugs. Lendax will be officially released at the event. And Professor Agnew is going to receive a prize for all his good work. He's going to retire soon."

"So if the professor can't help us, what can we do now?"

"We can inform the government office that licenses new drugs. Perhaps they'll investigate." Rick's anger was making him drive faster. "Maybe when they hear about . . ."

His voice stopped suddenly and his face turned gray.

"What is it?" Jess asked.

"The brakes! They're not working!"

Chapter 6

The next victim

"It's no good," he cried. "They're completely broken!" Every lane of the road was full. Lines of cars surrounded the jeep. Rick kicked at the brakes but nothing happened.

"Quick!" said Jess. "Where's the button for your warning lights?"

With the warning lights on, the traffic around them only grew slower. Rick was forced to drive dangerously from lane to lane as he turned between the vehicles.

"Stop!" shouted Jess. "Drive over to the side of the road."

"I'm trying!"

Jess screamed loudly as Rick got very close to the car in front. He had to try and avoid it so he turned directly in front of a bus. If they had been a few inches closer, they would have crashed. But finally the jeep rolled onto the side of the road. Small stones from the road's surface flew into the air. With Rick's foot off the gas, the jeep slowly stopped.

He sat in silence. He was breathing hard and staring at his shaking hands. Beside him, Jess was almost crying.

"What happened?" she asked.

Rick looked at the heavy traffic still rushing past. In his mind, he was feeling again all the terror of his previous crash. He shook his head to try to clear the memory.

"I'm not sure," he answered. "But I think that I can guess."

"I'm not surprised that your brakes aren't working," said the mechanic half an hour later. He was looking under the car, and his hands were covered in oil. "The brake fluid is completely empty. It's not even properly connected. And the light that should warn you if the fluid is low isn't connected either."

Rick looked at Jess and then turned back to the mechanic. "How could that happen?" he asked.

The mechanic shook his head. "Sometimes the pressure in the system can be very high. If the connections aren't tight, it can come loose. Or maybe a small stone on the road knocked it. It's bad luck. Especially since your warning light is loose as well. But give me a few minutes. I can fix this."

"Could someone have done this to my jeep on purpose?"

The man smiled. He thought it was a joke. Then he saw the look on Rick's face. "I suppose it's possible," he said. "It's possible to remove the connections. It's not the best way to make a car dangerous, but it's quick and it's easy."

Jess turned to Rick. "Maybe it was just a warning," she said.

The mechanic heard her. "There's no way of proving if this was done on purpose or not. But if you're serious, you need to tell the police."

As Rick drove back into town in his repaired jeep, he tried to think. He had secretly taken a few beta-blockers when Jess wasn't looking. The pills had helped, but the thought of the accident was making his heart speed again. Rick was sure that Victor Adams knew that Lendax was dangerous. And it was obvious that Adams didn't want Rick or Jess to tell anyone. So had Adams tried to kill them to keep them quiet? Had that enormous man, Patrick, done something to the jeep after he left Adams's office?

The possibility was terrible, and it gave Rick another terrible thought. *Maybe Will's death wasn't an accident either! Maybe Will discovered that Lendax isn't safe and he told Victor Adams. And maybe Adams then killed Will to make sure that he wouldn't tell anyone!*

After all, thought Rick, *Adams wants to sell Lendax all around the world. The market is worth millions and millions of dollars!*

The more Rick thought about it, the more it seemed possible. Patrick, the man who worked for Adams, seemed like a man who could kill. Will would not have had a chance against him. The thought made Rick afraid for Jess.

"Jess," he said. "It's not safe for you to be alone. I think you should collect your things and stay with me. There's plenty of room in my apartment."

"Are you sure?" asked Jess. Her reply was so quick that Rick realized she was thinking the same thing.

"Of course." He tried to smile. "It will cost you only half of the hotel rate," he joked.

Jess smiled for the first time that day.

Half an hour later, Rick was drinking coffee in his apartment and Jess was in the shower. His cell phone rang.

"Rick? It's Charles Agnew here. How was your meeting with Victor Adams?"

"He wouldn't tell us anything, Professor. I suggested that we should contact the other Lendax patients to warn them about the drug. But Adams just told us to leave. And there's more." Rick told Professor Agnew about the brakes on the jeep. "I'm sure that Adams is trying to hide the Lendax deaths. And I'm starting to suspect that Will's death wasn't an accident either. I think maybe he discovered that Lendax was dangerous and so Adams killed him."

"Rick! That's a very serious accusation. I know that Victor Adams is under a lot of pressure. It's true that his company would lose a lot of money if Lendax really is dangerous. But I can't believe that he would murder anyone."

"My brakes worked normally before I went to visit him," answered Rick. "And if I'm right about the drug, then Adams has an obvious reason for wanting us dead!"

"Rick, if you're sure that Victor Adams is doing something illegal, you must tell the police."

"I would," agreed Rick, "if I had one bit of proof. But so far all I know is that two patients have committed suicide. Unfortunately, that's not unusual. The police won't be interested."

"But your car . . . the brakes . . ."

"There's still no proof. It was made to look like an accident, just like Will's death. At the moment, I can't prove that Victor Adams is guilty."

There was silence as the professor thought. "I've got an idea," he said at last. "Why don't you speak to the newspapers? They would love a story like this. Victor Adams is releasing the drug at the East Coast Psychiatry Society conference tomorrow. If you talk to the newspapers about the Lendax trial and the deaths, they'll be very interested."

"Really?"

"Of course," said Agnew. "The newspapers love to write about the rich pharmaceutical companies who don't care about their patients. If they hear about a problem with Lendax, they'll cover their front pages with the story. Then the police would have to investigate. And the other patients taking Lendax would hear about it as well."

"That's a good idea," agreed Rick. "But you work for Tamsus, Professor. Do you really want to start working against them?"

"Rick, do you think I want to be involved with a company that cares so little for patients? If you're right, I'll be happy to stop working for Victor Adams."

Rick smiled. "I appreciate all your help, Professor. Let me discuss the idea with Jess. After all, it's her decision as well." Rick turned and saw Jess standing by the door. "I've got to go now, Professor."

"All right, Rick. Keep in touch."

As he hung up the phone, Jess sat on the sofa. Her large eyes looked up at Rick as she waited for him to explain the call.

"That was the professor," he said. "He thinks we should speak to the newspapers. If we tell everyone about the Lendax trial and your brother's death, the police will have to investigate."

Jess nodded. "That is a good idea. But there's another way," she said.

"What's that?" asked Rick. He sat down beside her on the sofa.

Jess turned to face him. "You could forget about all of this," she said.

"What?!"

"Listen, Rick. Adams doesn't want anyone to know that his drug is dangerous. He obviously wants to keep us quiet. This could get a lot worse for us both."

"But Jess . . ."

"I've lost Adrian already," she interrupted. "In a strange way, I was always prepared for that. He was taking Lendax because he had tried every other type of help. Nothing else worked and it was his last chance. He knew it was a risk but he tried the drug anyway. But you don't have to take risks yourself."

"Jess, companies like Tamsus spend millions of dollars every year advertising their products. When Victor Adams releases Lendax at the conference tomorrow, do you know how many patients could start taking that drug? Depression affects over 120 million people around the world! I'm not going to let all those people be tricked. I'm not going to let them take a drug that might be dangerous. And I'm not going to let Adams get even richer by selling a drug that might be dangerous!"

Rick reached over and took Jess's hand. "Adrian may have committed suicide," he continued. "But if Lendax is dangerous, then the people at Tamsus are to blame for his death. And they won't escape."

Jess nodded. She had a sad smile on her face. "Thank you," she said. She kissed him on the side of his face. There was an uncomfortable silence. Suddenly, Rick's cell phone rang.

"Hello?"

"Doctor Jamieson? It's Detective Anderson here."

"Hello, Detective," said Rick. "How can I help you?"

"Can you come and meet me?"

"Now?" Rick looked at his watch. "But it's almost eight o'clock!"

"I know. But we've found another of your Lendax patients. And he's dead."

Chapter 7

A suspect

When Rick arrived at the apartment by the North End Church, it was already dark outside. Two police cars were parked beside the building. Rick gave his name to a police officer and the man helped him through the small crowd on the sidewalk.

"Thank you for coming, Doctor Jamieson," said Detective Anderson, as Rick stepped through the open door. "His name is Gabriel Moranto. Forty-four years old."

"I don't recognize the name."

"We've checked with your boss. Mister Moranto was a patient at your clinic. There are Lendax syringes all over his bathroom."

"But I don't understand. If he's already dead, I can't help him."

"This will just take a few minutes, Doctor," said Detective Anderson.

"Where are we going?" asked Rick. The detective stared at him for a moment. Then Anderson pointed toward a room at the back of the apartment.

Gabriel Moranto was a large man. His body was still sitting at his kitchen table. His eyes were closed and his head was resting on the top of the table between his arms. There was a pool of blood on the floor. As Rick watched, the detective stepped forward and carefully pointed at the man's left arm.

"See the cuts?" asked Anderson. "His other arm is the same. And we found this on the floor."

The detective held up a bag. Inside was a large kitchen knife. The sight made Rick feel very sad.

"What do you think happened?" asked the detective.

"It's clear, isn't it?" answered Rick. "Mister Moranto cut himself. He then probably fainted from the loss of blood. And finally his heart must have stopped."

"How do you know that he cut himself?"

Rick looked closely at the body. "Look at the line of the cuts," he said. "That confirms that he did it to himself." He pointed at the man's left arm. "And the cuts are deeper here. He was probably right-handed."

"Very good," nodded the detective. "As you say, it was clearly done on purpose."

As Anderson continued to speak about the death, Rick felt more and more uncomfortable. He was beginning to feel the signs of a panic attack. He started to sweat. His sight began to spin and his heart beat faster.

He needed to take a beta-blocker, but he didn't want Detective Anderson to see.

"Excuse me," he said. He hurried toward the front door. His hands searched quickly in his pocket for his pills.

The detective arrived as Rick was replacing the beta-blockers in the pocket of his pants. "Are you not feeling well, Doctor?" he asked. "Your face is a little gray." Rick wondered if Anderson had seen the pills.

"I just wanted some air," said Rick. He took a few deep breaths. "So tell me, Detective. Why am I here?"

"Why do you think you're here?" replied Anderson. "Is there anything you want to tell me?"

"Well," Rick began, "Mister Moranto has committed suicide, just like Adrian Blake and Anna Richards. That seems to be the problem with Lendax. The drug doesn't help. Instead, it gives the patients just enough energy to kill themselves."

The detective shook his head. "I mean is there anything you want to tell me about yourself?"

Rick looked up at the man, at his large body and the face that never smiled. "All right," he nodded slowly. "I went out to Milton this afternoon with Jessica Blake, Adrian's sister. I went to speak to the people at Tamsus, the company behind Lendax."

The detective looked impressed. "You just walked straight into their office?"

"Professor Charles Agnew helped us. He's an old friend and teacher of mine. The professor works for Tamsus. He arranged a meeting for us with the boss, Victor Adams."

"I know all about Adams. He's a friend of the Police Commissioner. Adams is connected in some way to every important person in Boston. So what did you say to him?"

"I told him about the suicides. I said that it was his duty to stop the Lendax release tomorrow. And I told him that he should test the drug again. Because, at the moment, he can't guarantee that the drug is safe."

"And what did Adams say to you?"

Rick sighed. "He threw us out of his office."

"That sounds like Victor Adams," nodded Anderson. The Tamsus boss was obviously not his favorite person.

"That's not all," added Rick. "Our brakes failed on the way

back. They were working on the way to Milton. But after an hour in the Tamsus parking lot, we suddenly had a problem. We almost had a very dangerous accident on the way home."

"Did you have the vehicle checked?"

"Of course. Unfortunately it's impossible to prove that it wasn't just an accident. But there's something else . . ."

"What's that, Doctor?"

"The other doctor at my clinic, Will Sutton. He died a few weeks ago when he was climbing in Adirondack Park. I think that maybe his death wasn't an accident either."

The detective looked surprised. "Why do you think that?"

"When the Lendax trial started, Will was the doctor in charge. Maybe he discovered that the drug isn't safe. Maybe he told Victor Adams what he had found. And maybe Adams killed him to keep him quiet."

"That's quite an idea, Doctor Jamieson."

"Will you investigate it? Please?"

The detective looked thoughtful. "All right. I'll look at the report on Doctor Sutton's death. You can go back home now. I'll call you tomorrow."

Rick walked toward the door. Then suddenly, he turned round again. "One last thing, Detective," he said. "Why did you want me to come here tonight?"

Detective Anderson stepped closer to Rick until they were face to face. "I'll investigate Doctor Sutton's death, like I said," he answered. "And I'll contact Victor Adams and ask him for the names of the other patients. But let me make this clear." He nodded toward the kitchen. "Mister Moranto is the third patient to have died."

"I know. I told you. Lendax isn't safe."

"Maybe that's true. Or maybe that's what I'm meant to think."

"What do you mean?"

"I've got three dead bodies," Detective Anderson said. "One died from high levels of Lendax. One fell out of a window. And Mister Moranto here has been badly cut. But there's no actual proof that they killed themselves. In fact, I've now spoken to a few people who knew the three dead patients. And they've all told me that the patients were getting better."

It took Rick a moment to understand what Detective Anderson was saying. He was amazed. "Do you think that all these patients were *murdered*?"

"I don't know yet. But I asked you to come here tonight for a reason. I need to investigate every connection between these patients. Lendax connects them, of course. But there's also one person connected to all of these patients through the clinic. Someone who can make murder look like suicide. Someone I found at the scene of Adrian Blake's death. And someone who I see is taking pills himself. The same person who would try to waste my time with talk of brakes and climbing accidents. It could be you, Doctor Jamieson!"

As the cab took him home, Rick looked out at the Boston streets. His mind was turning round and round. The news that he was a suspect was shocking.

I don't even know the names of the people involved in the trial, he thought. *And I certainly don't have a reason to kill them. It's obvious that Tamsus is to blame. Their new drug is dangerous! It isn't helping patients. Instead, it's pushing them to commit suicide. And now Victor Adams is trying to make sure that he doesn't lose millions of dollars of profit. He's trying to hide his company's failure. And he isn't afraid to kill everyone who knows about it.*

Rick stepped out of the cab and approached the front door to his apartment building. He was very tired, but the idea of seeing Jess again excited him. Something strange had happened between them earlier. She had looked so helpless and her face so full of pain. He had wanted to protect her. In a strange way, he felt stronger beside her. And then she had kissed him . . .

He made his way to the second floor and turned the lock on his front door. When he stepped inside, he noticed the darkness immediately. It wasn't very late, but all the lights were off. The whole apartment was black.

"Jess?" he called. When there was no answer, he began to panic. Had Adams found her already? Was she hurt?

"Jess?" he called again louder.

Rick ran through the apartment. As he hurried toward the bedroom at the back, he turned on every light and shouted her name. He pushed open the bedroom door and reached for the light switch. For a few seconds, Rick stood frozen. He felt sick with fear. Jess's body lay across the bed. Her eyes were closed and her body was still.

Chapter 8

Patients or profits?

"Jess!" cried Rick. He ran to her and shook her hard. "Jess!"

Jess sighed in her sleep. Rick felt weak with relief. As she opened her eyes, she saw him and she smiled. "Is everything all right?" she asked.

Rick forced himself to hide the fear that he had felt. "Everything's fine," he smiled. "Go back to sleep."

Jess nodded and closed her eyes. As her breathing calmed, Rick rose to turn off the light. The sickness had gone. Instead, he just felt very tired.

In the gray light, Jess looked so peaceful. Rick sat beside her and gently pushed the long dark hair from her face. She seemed so strong in herself. But now she was relying on him to feel safe. He felt a strange mix of responsibility and happiness. And then the tiredness hit him again.

A quick shower, he thought. *And then I'll go to bed.*

As he rose to go, Jess reached out in her sleep. She caught his hand and held it close. Rick looked at her and smiled and she pulled him near her. *I suppose a shower can wait a few more minutes,* he thought.

Hours later, Rick woke up. The bed beside him was empty. A moment later, Jess appeared.

"Good morning," she smiled.

Rick was embarrassed. He was still wearing his clothes

from the day before. "I'm sorry. I was so tired last night. I must have fallen asleep."

"Don't worry," she said. "It was nice to have you beside me. I didn't enjoy being here alone while you were out last night." She held out a cup of coffee. "So what happened with Detective Anderson?"

Rick took the coffee and sighed. "I saw the third Lendax victim," he said. "The man had cut himself with a knife. It was terrible."

Jess covered her open mouth with a hand. "But why did Anderson ask you to meet him there?"

"He wanted to see how I would react."

"What do you mean?"

"Anderson has agreed to question Victor Adams about the Lendax trial," he said. "But the detective thinks that maybe the patients didn't kill themselves."

"I don't understand."

"Anderson thinks that they might have been murdered."

Jess shook her head. The idea was obviously very difficult for her. "But why would anyone want to murder Adrian?"

"I don't know. It makes no sense to me. Anderson is going to investigate Tamsus, but he thinks someone else is to blame."

"Who?" asked Jess.

"Me."

"What? You? Why would Anderson think that?" she said angrily.

"Because he thinks that I know how to hide the signs of murder. And because he found me in Adrian's apartment. And all the victims are from my clinic."

"But what about your brakes? And Will's death? What did he say about that?"

"He said that I could be trying to waste his time."

"I don't believe it!"

"There's another reason that Anderson thinks I might be dangerous." Rick stopped, embarrassed.

"What?"

Rick swallowed. "I'm taking pills myself. Anderson saw me taking them last night."

"What sort of pills?" asked Jess. When Rick didn't answer, she tried again. "Rick? What sort of pills?"

"It's nothing to worry about," he said. "They're called beta-blockers. A few years ago, I was in a road accident. I broke my right leg, my left arm, and a few other smaller bones. I was trapped inside my car for several hours. Finally, they had to cut me out of the vehicle. Now I suffer from panic attacks when I'm in a small space or when I feel stress."

"That's why you didn't use the elevator at Tamsus!"

"I don't want you to think that I'm weak. That's why I didn't tell you. No one knows about the pills except Anderson. It doesn't mean that I'm dangerous." Rick tried to smile. "Believe me, Jess. I take pills because I don't like small spaces, not because I'm a murderer."

"I understand." Jess took Rick's hand. Her blue eyes were full of concern. "It must have been terrible for you yesterday when the brakes didn't work."

"It was. But I'm fine. There's nothing to worry about."

"Good. Well, I won't worry about Detective Anderson either. He'll soon realize that he's wrong. But what about the other Lendax patients? We still don't know who they are. They deserve to be warned."

Rick looked at his watch. "You're right," he said. "I should go to work now anyway. I'll speak to Kramer again. I'm sure he'll give me the trial details now."

"All right," nodded Jess. "Do you mind if I stay here again tonight? The hotel doesn't feel safe."

"Of course. You can stay as long as you like," said Rick.

"Thank you, Rick. You've been very kind to me."

Rick smiled. "I'd better get to work."

"Maybe you should take a shower first?"

"There's no time. I'm going to be late as it is."

"OK. I'll call you later. And Rick?"

"Yes?"

Jess gave him a warm smile. "I don't think you're weak."

When Rick arrived at the clinic, he went straight to Kramer's office.

"Ian," he said. "I need to speak to you about . . ."

"And I need to speak to you!" Kramer interrupted angrily. "A detective, a guy called Anderson, contacted me yesterday evening. He wanted to talk about you and the Lendax trial. He told me that you're a possible murder suspect!"

"It's nothing to worry about, Ian. I promise you." Rick began to explain. "Three patients involved in the Lendax trial have committed suicide recently, so I visited Tamsus and spoke to Victor Adams . . ."

"What?!" shouted Kramer. "Rick, I told you! This is nothing to do with you. It's not unusual for depressed patients to kill themselves. You had no right to bother Adams."

"But the other patients on Lendax have a right to know about the deaths! They might be in danger. And when I told Adams that he should stop the trial, he threw me out of his office."

"Of course he did! Lendax has already passed all the tests. The drug is safe. It's terrible that three patients have killed themselves. But there are lots of other patients around the world who can benefit from Lendax!"

"But there's more, Ian. On the way home, my brakes failed. I could have been killed. I think Adams may be to blame."

"Have you any proof?"

"No, it was made to look like an accident."

"Or perhaps it was just an accident!" said Kramer loudly.

"It made me realize something," answered Rick. He was determined to continue. "Maybe Will's death wasn't an accident either. Maybe Will discovered that Lendax is dangerous and so he was murdered."

"Rick," replied Kramer, "Victor Adams is head of one of the biggest pharmaceutical companies in the world. Do you really think that he would murder his own patients and make his own drug look dangerous?"

"I know it's difficult to believe but . . ."

"It's impossible to believe," interrupted Kramer. "And you still haven't explained why Detective Anderson thinks that you're a murderer."

Rick sighed. "Because he found me at Adrian's apartment. And because I'm linked to all the victims through this clinic. It's nothing to worry about," he added. "Anderson is just investigating every possible idea."

"Rick, I do worry. I worry when you leave work early, as

you did yesterday. I worry when policemen arrive to question me about my staff. I worry when I hear that one of my staff is a murder suspect. And most importantly, I worry that the pharmaceutical companies will hear that one of my staff is a murder suspect!"

There was a bitter smile on Rick's face. "I understand now," he said. "You're not worried about me or the other Lendax patients at all. You just don't want to upset your pharmaceutical friends. For you, this isn't about helping patients. For you, this is just business."

"Grow up, Rick!" shouted Kramer. "Whether you like it or not, we rely on the pharmaceutical companies. Without them, there would be no drugs at all. Those companies pay us for every trial. And without the trials, we couldn't afford new drugs. Maybe you should think about that before you start making up stories!"

There was a silence as both men stared at each other. Then Kramer took a deep breath. "Look," he continued, "Tamsus is supporting the conference this afternoon. This is a huge opportunity for us. Tamsus make lots of different drugs, not just antidepressants. If the conference goes well, they will guarantee us a cheap supply of their drugs. And that's good for our patients. We need to be friends with the large companies like Tamsus. But they won't do business with a murder suspect. And I can't let you accuse them of murder either!"

"I understand," nodded Rick. "But I still think we need to warn the other Lendax patients."

"Rick, this discussion is over. The conference starts in a few hours, so I'm leaving soon. Just stay here and continue with your work."

"But Ian . . ."

"Get to work!"

Rick returned to his office. He was very angry. After all, he was only trying to do what was right.

Maybe I'm wrong, he thought. *Perhaps the problem with my jeep was just an accident. And maybe it's just bad luck that three Lendax patients have killed themselves. Maybe the drug isn't to blame.*

For a moment, Rick considered doing what Kramer had told him. *I could forget about the trial,* he thought. The idea was tempting. *If Lendax already has a license, why should I worry? Maybe we should just take the money from Tamsus and not ask any questions. After all, every clinic needs money to buy drugs.*

But then Rick thought of Jess and Adrian. *What would I do if things were different? If another patient had died instead of Adrian, I would want to warn Jess and her brother. Adrian would have a right to know. And it would be my duty to tell him.*

Rick made up his mind. He had to get the details of the other trial patients. Even without proof, he had to warn them that Lendax might be dangerous.

But I've still got the same problem! he realized. *All the details for the Lendax trial are on Kramer's computer and I don't have the password!*

Rick sat at his desk and thought carefully. *There has to be a way! If I can't contact the other patients, they might all end up like Adrian.*

Suddenly, Rick smiled. "Of course! Adrian is the answer," he said out loud.

Rick had learned about Adrian from a program on Will's computer. The program told him when his patients needed more drugs.

If the computer told me about Adrian, he thought, *perhaps it can tell me about other Lendax patients too!*

As quickly as possible, Rick opened Will's files. He soon found the list of prescriptions with Adrian's name near the top. Near the very end, he saw the word "Lendax" again. And beside the name of the drug was the name of another patient: Sebastian Doyle, age 56.

I've found one! thought Rick. *And maybe Sebastian Doyle can tell me about some of the other patients!*

Rick picked up the phone but then he paused. *This is too important to talk about on the phone,* he thought. *I should visit Sebastian Doyle and tell him everything, face to face.*

The file said that Sebastian Doyle lived on a street in Charlestown. Rick could be there in fifteen minutes and return within an hour. Kramer would never know that Rick had left.

He was leaving his office when the telephone rang.

"Rick? It's Jess. Have you spoken to your boss?"

"Yes. He refused to give me any details about the trial. But I've found the name of another Lendax patient. He lives in Charlestown. I'm going there now. I'm going to warn him that Lendax isn't safe."

"Do you want me to come?"

Rick thought quickly. "No. You should go and see Professor Agnew. If the police won't believe me, they'll believe him. He'll be preparing for the conference at the Conference Center. Tell him that Lendax has killed a third patient. I'm sure that he'll support us. I'll call you later."

Chapter 9

Trapped

The street in Charlestown was similar to where Adrian had lived on Beacon Hill.

It's hard to believe that I found Adrian's body just two days ago, thought Rick. The memory now made him angry.

Drug trials are meant to improve life, he thought. *They are supposed to create hope. Instead, Victor Adams is playing with the lives of patients. Adams doesn't care about people. He only cares about money.*

Rick approached Sebastian Doyle's apartment block. He was determined to tell Doyle everything. Kramer couldn't stop him. Rick knew that he was doing the right thing.

An old woman was leaving as he arrived. She smiled and held open the front door.

"Thank you," said Rick. A list of names on the wall showed who lived in the building. Sebastian Doyle was in apartment 12 on the fourth floor.

The elevator was directly ahead. He thought of stepping into the small space and immediately felt nervous. Rick stared at the elevator for a moment. His heart began to race, and he felt foolish. After all, he was an adult. He was a doctor. He knew there was no reason to be afraid. But still he turned toward the stairs.

A few minutes later, he arrived at the top of the building and pushed through a heavy fire door into a corridor. As he stepped through the door, he saw a shadow moving up ahead, by the elevator. Someone had stepped quickly out of the corridor. The elevator doors began to close.

Rick walked closer. Suddenly, he realized that apartment 12 was opposite the elevator. And the door to the apartment was open. The person in the elevator must have just left.

"Mister Doyle?" Rick called along the corridor. *Maybe that's Sebastian Doyle in the elevator,* thought Rick. *Maybe he's going out. But then why would he leave his apartment door open?* Rick's heart jumped as he remembered Detective Anderson's idea. *Maybe the patients aren't killing themselves. Maybe someone is murdering them. And maybe the person in the elevator is the murderer!*

Rick started to run, but the elevator was already going down. The person inside was escaping. But what could Rick do? He could try to catch the person. But if Rick took the stairs, he would be too late. And maybe Sebastian Doyle was inside the apartment. Maybe Doyle needed urgent help.

Rick's heart was racing as he stepped through the open door of number 12.

"Hello?" he called. "Mister Doyle?"

An image of Adrian's dead body appeared in Rick's mind. His hands began to shake. The lights were on in the apartment. On a table by the door were some keys.

Rick moved further into the apartment, nervously. He didn't know what he was going to find.

"Mister Doyle?" he shouted again into the silence. There was still no answer.

Rick found himself in an empty living room. Beyond a large sofa there was a door to the kitchen. Beside that, by the far wall, was an enormous glass dining table. The table was covered in books and papers and boxes.

12

"Hello?" Rick called quietly. He was almost afraid of an answer.

It was only when he saw the stairs that he noticed Sebastian Doyle. Rick approached slowly, his heart heavy with pity.

Above the stairs, the man's body was hanging from his neck. His face was gray. His eyes were wide open. They stared across the room. There was no doubt in Rick's mind. The man was dead.

Rick stepped closer. He couldn't believe it. He was only a few minutes too late. Rick's body began to shake and he turned away. It was then that he noticed the Lendax. Among the books and the papers, half a dozen syringes were spread across the table.

This is like the other deaths, he thought. *It looks like another suicide. But maybe Detective Anderson was right! Maybe there is more to this than a dangerous drug.*

Someone had left the apartment as Rick arrived. *Could that person have murdered Doyle and the other patients?* he wondered. *And why would anyone want to kill them?*

He stepped closer to the body. He was looking for signs of a struggle when a deep voice came from behind.

"Doctor Jamieson. What a surprise."

Rick turned quickly. Detective Anderson stood by the corridor. A uniformed police officer was by his side.

"Detective!" said Rick shocked. "Why are you here?"

"I'm doing my job. I'm just sorry it took me so long."

"What do you mean?"

"Doctor Jamieson, I'm arresting you for murder."

"What?! But I just arrived here. I found him like this."

"So how did you get into the apartment?" It was clear that he didn't trust Rick at all.

"The door was open."

"How convenient," nodded Anderson. "Just like Adrian Blake's front door, I suppose. And the outside door to the apartment block? Was that open, too?"

"There was an old woman. She let me in." Rick knew his answers sounded bad.

"So, once again, you're at the scene of a murder. And you're standing over the body of a dead patient."

"There was someone else here in the apartment," said Rick. "I came to warn Mister Doyle about Lendax. But as I arrived, someone else was leaving. I saw that person run into the elevator."

Detective Anderson obviously didn't believe Rick. "We didn't see anyone," he said.

"But . . . but how did you get here?" asked Rick. "Where did you get this address?"

"I'd like to know where you got this address. You told me that you have no details of the trial volunteers. And yet here you are."

"I had another look on the clinic's computer. I found this one name and address. What about you?"

"Victor Adams finally gave me a list of all the patients in the trial. I got it this morning and came to check on Mister Doyle here." Anderson nodded at the hanging body and held up a piece of printed paper. "This list names the twenty people who agreed to take part in Doctor Will Sutton's trial. And Mister Doyle here is the fifth victim."

"Fifth?" asked Rick. "But there are only four."

Anderson's face was suddenly full of anger. "You know that there are five!" he shouted. "Elizabeth Wiley." He banged the list down on the table. "She was found just two weeks ago. That was very clever of you, Doctor. She was lying dead in her bath beside her electric radio. It could have been an accident, or it could have been suicide. Or it could have been murder."

Rick's heart jumped. His sight began to spin. He couldn't believe what he was hearing. So many people were dead, and the detective thought that Rick was responsible. As the police officer stepped closer, he felt like a trapped animal. "Please," he said, "my beta-blockers. They're in my pocket. Let me take some."

Anderson nodded and the police officer removed the bottle of pills from Rick's pocket. Rick quickly swallowed two beta-blockers. Then, with shaking hands, he looked at the paper that Anderson had left on the table.

"Private," the paper read. "The property of Tamsus Plc. Lendax trial, Boston." There was a long list of the Tamsus doctors involved in the trial and then the name "Doctor William Sutton." Then there was a line of patient names. After each one was an age and an address. Some of the names were familiar. Adrian Blake's was near the top. Several lines below that, he read the name "Elizabeth Wiley," then "Gabriel Moranto." A few lines below that was "Anna Richards." And near the bottom of the list, Rick read the name "Sebastian Doyle."

All five patients had needed help. And all five of them were now dead. Even the doctor managing the trial, Rick's friend Will Sutton, was dead. But why?

"Did you investigate Will's accident?" Rick asked Anderson.

"I did," replied the detective. "And I discovered that Will Sutton received two phone calls on the morning he died.

The first was from you and the second was from Professor Agnew's office. The professor has already told me that he was discussing the Lendax trial. So what did you discuss?"

"Will and I were going to meet that evening for drinks. I called him to confirm, but he was . . ." Suddenly, Rick remembered something. A memory deep in his mind was shouting to him. "The professor!" he said. "Professor Agnew told you that he spoke to Will that morning from his office?"

Detective Anderson nodded. "They discussed the trial. That seems normal to me. After all, Agnew was one of the Tamsus doctors involved."

"What?"

"Look at the list."

A drop of sweat fell from Rick's face. He looked again at the list. And there, near the top, was the professor's name. "But Professor Agnew told me that he wasn't involved!" Rick said. "And he told me that he was away on the day that Will died. He said that he was in California!"

Chapter 10

Escape

"It was him!" cried Rick. "It must have been the professor!" He held up the list. "There's his name: Professor Charles Agnew. He was involved in the trial, and he had access to all the patients."

Detective Anderson was not impressed. He shook his head. "So now you're telling me that the people at Tamsus are killing their own patients? That's difficult to believe." Anderson turned to the police officer beside him. "Officer Parker, why don't you help Doctor Jamieson downstairs? We'll continue this conversation at the police station."

"Look," Rick shouted, as the police officer stepped closer. "You have to believe me! Agnew told me that he wasn't involved in the trial. Why would he hide that from me?"

"To be honest, Doctor, I don't care," replied Anderson. "But we'll have plenty of time to talk later." As Parker stepped closer, Rick had another terrible thought. Jess was on her way to meet Agnew! Rick had sent her to talk to the professor. She was going to tell him everything that they knew. If Agnew thought that he was close to discovery, the professor might kill her as well. And it would be Rick's fault. He had to help her. He had to escape from the police and find Agnew before Jess got hurt.

As the police officer reached toward him, Rick raised his hands. "Wait," he said, his voice weak. "My pills aren't working. I feel . . ." As he spoke, Rick pretended to lose his balance. He fell back toward the table. Parker stepped forward to take his arm. As the police officer reached for him, Rick twisted round. In his hand was one of the Lendax syringes. Before the police officer could react, Rick was holding the syringe against the man's neck.

Immediately, Detective Anderson pulled out his gun. "Don't move, Doctor," he shouted. "Put the syringe down and turn around!"

But Rick had already stepped behind Parker. He slipped his other arm around the police officer's neck and held him tight.

"I'm sorry," said Rick, "but I've got no choice."

"Doctor!" shouted Anderson again. "Put the syringe down and let him go! You won't escape from here!"

Rick carefully pressed the syringe against the police officer's neck. "Detective Anderson," he said, "I want you to slowly put your gun on the floor. Then I want you to get down on your knees and face the corner." Rick nodded toward the far side of the room.

Anderson shook his head. "No," he said. The detective was still pointing his gun at Rick's head. "If what you're saying is true, then the Lendax isn't dangerous. You're trying to trick me."

Rick nodded. "You're right, Detective. Lendax isn't dangerous in the arm or the leg. But if I empty this syringe into this man's neck, the drug will go straight to his heart. The shock will kill him. So do as I say!"

Anderson was very angry but he slowly got down on his knees.

"I really am sorry about this," Rick repeated. He pulled the police officer toward the apartment door. As he passed the table, he picked up the keys. "It would take too long to persuade you," he said. "Jess Blake is in trouble and it's my fault. I have to help her."

Rick suddenly pushed the police officer away and then ran out through the door. He quickly closed it behind him, locked it, and threw down the keys.

On the other side of the door, Detective Anderson was shouting. "Don't be a fool, Doctor."

But Rick was already running towards the stairs. His mind was fixed only on Jess.

The East Coast Psychiatry Society was meeting in the Conference Center of Harvard Medical School, on the south side of the city. That was where Agnew would be, and where Jess had gone to find him. Rick ran past the empty police car parked outside the building and he continued down the sidewalk. He was angry with himself. He had sent Jess to Agnew. He had pushed her toward the danger instead of protecting her. He had to save her and he had to hurry.

Behind him, the sound of police alarms rose and fell. "I should have taken Anderson's radio," he thought, as he turned quickly into a side street.

The police were now hunting for him. Detective Anderson must have called others to help. In just a few minutes, Rick's details would be all over Boston. Every police officer in the city would be looking for him.

As Rick ran down the side street, he pulled off his coat and threw it away. The change wouldn't help much, but from a distance it might give him a few extra seconds. At the end of the street, the road north was full of cars. They were moving slowly in a long line. Suddenly, he heard the sound of a police car. It appeared quickly around the corner. Rick forced himself to stop. He pretended to look in the window of a shop as the car raced past. It was going away from him, toward Sebastian Doyle's apartment.

Rick looked up and down the street. His luck was good; in the line of traffic was an empty cab. He ran forward, opened the door, and jumped inside.

"Harvard Medical School!" he shouted to the driver. "As quick as you can. It's off Brookline Avenue."

"I know where it is!" the driver shouted back. She switched off the radio and turned into the traffic moving south. "Hold on tight," she shouted, as another police car rushed past in the opposite direction. "We'll be there in ten minutes."

One block from the Conference Center, Rick stopped the cab. Detective Anderson knew that he was looking for Agnew. The police were probably already waiting to stop him at the door.

But Rick had been to many lectures at the Conference Center. He knew the building well. He walked quickly round to the kitchen doors at the back. As he approached, a small group of men and women were walking in and out. They were carrying plates full of food. Rick waited until some people were entering together. Then he walked forward with them and stepped inside. No one stopped him. A few seconds later, he was climbing the stairs up toward the entrance hall.

But where will Agnew be? he wondered. The professor worked for Tamsus, and he was at the conference to receive an important prize. As the star guest, he would be a popular man. Maybe Kramer was looking after him? After all, Kramer was organizing the conference. Or maybe Jess had already found him, and Agnew had taken her somewhere else? Maybe Rick was too late.

No, he thought. *I can't think like that. I have to find her.*

As he climbed the stairs, he could hear the noise of all the people talking loudly in the front hall. *There must be hundreds of them!* he thought. *How will I find Agnew or Jess among so many people?*

Rick could now see into the entrance hall. A large crowd covered the whole area. He couldn't see more than a few feet in any direction.

I've got to keep climbing, he realized. There was a smaller, second floor above the hall. It ran around the side of the building. *I'll be able to find them from up there.*

He hurried on to the second floor, then stepped out and walked slowly to the edge. He looked around the large crowd, but he couldn't see either Agnew or Jess. In one corner, Kramer was talking to a group of people. In the middle of the group, a small man wearing glasses was nodding as he listened. It was Victor Adams.

Kramer began to lead the group toward the main conference hall. With a proud smile, he was making a path through the crowd. And then, by chance, he looked up and saw Rick. Immediately, Kramer looked very angry. And then Rick's boss forced himself to smile. Kramer turned back to Victor Adams and said a few words. Adams nodded, and then Kramer looked up again at Rick. He began to push his way through the crowd. He was moving toward the stairs.

Kramer's going to tell me to leave! realized Rick. *I haven't got time to explain everything. I've got to escape from him and find Jess.*

Suddenly, Rick had an idea. On the floor above, there were private rooms. People used them to prepare for the conferences. *Agnew must be up there,* thought Rick. *It's the only place I haven't looked.*

But Kramer was coming up the stairs. If Rick went back that way, Kramer would catch him. There was only one other way.

On the far side of the floor was the Conference Center elevator. Rick ran round quickly and pressed the button. Instantly, the door opened. He took a deep breath and stepped inside. As Rick pressed the button for the top floor, Kramer appeared at the top of the stairs. Rick saw him shouting, but he didn't hear the words. He couldn't think. He could hardly breathe. The elevator door was closing fast.

Rick's heart was banging in his chest. He could hear it. His body was covered in sweat and he felt sicker than ever before. He felt trapped again, just as he had been in the car crash eighteen months before. With a jump, the elevator started to move. Rick's legs felt weak. He put his hands on the wall to steady himself. The walls seemed to be sliding closer. Rick clearly remembered the pain of the car crash. It made him want to scream. With shaking hands, he reached into his pocket for his pills. In his panic, he almost dropped the bottle. At last, he managed to open it. He didn't bother to count the pills but just poured them into his mouth.

I have to do this! I have to help Jess! He shut his eyes and forced himself to breathe slowly. Finally, the elevator stopped. The doors slowly opened and Rick stepped out on shaking legs. He was on the top floor.

He still felt faint and his heart was beating fast. In his ears, he could hear a sound like a strong wind. As the sound calmed, he began to feel more normal. And then he noticed the voices. Above the noise of all the people far below at the bottom of the building, he could hear Jess. She wasn't far away, and she sounded angry. Then he heard an answer and he knew that she was talking to Agnew.

Slowly, with his body still shaking, he began to walk toward them as quietly as possible.

Chapter 11

The final trial

The voices grew louder. Rick passed the doors to the private rooms, but they were empty. He continued toward a corner in the corridor.

They must be in the gallery, thought Rick.

The gallery was the platform high above the main conference hall. There was only one entrance, and the walls were covered in handles and buttons. They operated the enormous lights above the hall. Rick could hear Agnew and Jess clearly now. They were just around the corner.

"I don't believe you!" Jess was crying.

"Jessica," Agnew replied, "you must trust me. I know this is difficult to believe, but it's true. And I blame myself. I took so long to realize. But Rick is the murderer. He's ill."

"But he doesn't seem . . ."

"That's why it has taken us so long to realize," interrupted Agnew. "Rick knows how to hide the signs of his illness. He can hide the signs because he sees patients with those same signs every day. You must believe me! Rick is dangerous. He's been tricking us all. Rick is the murderer."

"But why?" asked Jess. "Rick's a good man. Why would he want to kill his patients?"

Rick stepped around the corner. "I'd like to hear your answer to that, Professor," he said.

For only an instant, Agnew stood motionless and silent.

Then he recovered and smiled. "Rick," he said. His voice was very calm. "What are you doing here?"

Suddenly, Rick felt more tired than ever. The sight of his old teacher made him very sad. "I've come to tell you that it's over," he said. "I know what you've done, and the police aren't far behind me."

"Really?" Agnew was still smiling, but he looked quickly down into the hall far below. It was still empty; the conference hadn't started. "Tell me, what have I done?"

It was the smile that made Rick so angry. Agnew didn't seem to care about all the deaths. "You're a doctor!" Rick shouted as he stepped forward along the gallery. "You made a promise to help your patients. But instead you killed them." Rick had respected his old friend and teacher. But now that respect had turned to disgust.

The professor began to step back, circling away from Rick. He was silent for several seconds. It was as though he was making a decision. Then suddenly, he laughed. "You really think that doctors can help everyone, don't you?" Agnew said. "But I'll tell you what my years of work have taught me. No one can beat depression. Not even us."

Jess stared at the professor. She began to shake her head violently from side to side.

Agnew turned to look at her. "I saw your brother several times, Jessica," he said. His voice was still calm. He showed no emotion, but slowly continued to circle away. "Adrian was very unhappy. I helped him to escape. Is that so bad?"

"You killed him!" Tears appeared in Jess's eyes as Rick stepped forward. He knew that the professor was moving closer to the only exit, but he didn't care. Agnew would never be able to escape. "Adrian was ill," Rick said. "They were all ill. They were depressed. They couldn't think clearly. So how can you claim to know what they wanted?"

"Because I've listened to people like them every day for thirty-five years!" shouted Agnew. Suddenly, his anger had burst free. "I've listened to my patients. They tell us that they have no hope. So what do we do? We tell them that the drugs will help. And so they take the drugs and they wait for all their problems to disappear. But, of course, their problems don't disappear. Instead, the same patients return to us for help, day after day and year after year."

"Do you expect me to believe that, Professor?" said Rick. "That you're some sort of mercy killer? That you became a murderer to *help* people?"

"No, Rick," replied Agnew. He shook his head like a disappointed father. "I became a murderer because I thought it was time for me to get rich as well."

There was a confused silence. "I don't understand," said Rick. "You work for Tamsus. And if people think that their drug is dangerous, they'll only suffer. The value of their company will fall. No one would benefit except . . ." Rick's face turned pale. "Of course!" he said.

"What is it?" asked Jess.

Rick stared at Agnew. "There are two major pharmaceutical companies in North America," he said. "One is Tamsus, the other is called Trodan. Almost half of all the drugs sold around the world come from those two companies. Together, they control a world market worth over two hundred and fifty billion dollars."

Jess shook her head. "So?"

"If the Lendax release is delayed, Trodan will control the market. They can release their own antidepressant without competition. The company will make millions. Won't they, Professor?"

Agnew said nothing. But his eyes were shining with pleasure, like a teacher with his favorite student.

"So Trodan is behind this," said Jess. "Did Trodan pay you to kill my brother, Professor?"

Agnew smiled. "The people at Trodan know nothing about this. When they learned about Tamsus's new drug, they were very worried. The value of their company fell quickly. Only I thought of a way to take advantage of the situation . . ."

"You invested in Trodan when prices were at their lowest," said Rick.

"Correct!" smiled the professor. "You always were a good student. I put all the money I could find into Trodan. And now the Lendax launch will be delayed. Trodan will soon release their own antidepressant without competition, and the value of their company will climb higher than ever before."

"And you'll make millions of dollars!" said Rick.

"Correct again," Agnew said. "And the people at Trodan will be very grateful as well. After all, it's their business to make money."

"It's their business to help people, not to kill them," answered Rick.

The professor laughed. "You're always so innocent, Rick! Pharmaceutical companies aren't really interested in helping people," he said. "Money is the most important thing for them, not health. Together, Tamsus and Trodan made profits last year of more than twenty-five billion dollars. Did they use that money to help more patients? Of course not!"

"It's not a crime to make money. But it is a crime to kill. And the police will be here soon, Professor."

Agnew looked carefully at his old friend. "Are they coming for me, Rick, or for you?"

Rick hesitated and looked quickly at Jess. It was for only a second, but it was enough.

The professor laughed again. Rick looked at him in horror. He knew that it would be hard to convince the police that it was Agnew who was the murderer and not him.

"The brakes!" realized Rick. "You damaged the brakes on my jeep!"

"But you ignored it," said Agnew. "And so, because of you, this became a murder case. Now you can share the blame."

"You . . . !"

"Yes, Rick," said Agnew. "When the police search your office later, they will find a large amount of Lendax in your desk. Everyone will think that you are taking the drug as well. I can imagine the newspapers tomorrow: 'Doctor takes new drug and then kills his patients and himself.' What a terrible shock for Tamsus! Their new drug will not be popular," smiled Agnew. "And what a good time for me to retire."

"And Will," said Rick. "You killed Will as well, didn't you?"

Agnew looked almost sorry. "I asked Will to manage the Lendax trial. I admit that it was a mistake. After the first death, Will started to suspect that something was wrong. He was going to tell the police. And, of course, I couldn't let him do that. So . . ."

"Will became victim number two . . ." finished Rick.

His voice was now full of anger. "All those people here today . . . they trusted you," he said. "They were going to give you a prize for all the good you have done. But you're nothing. You're just a murderer. And you're not going to escape."

"You're wrong, Rick," answered Agnew. "*You* are not going to escape." He held out an arm. In his hand he held a syringe of Lendax.

Suddenly Rick realized. There was no way past Agnew. The professor wasn't moving toward the exit because he wanted to get away. He wanted to make sure that Rick and Jess didn't get away!

Jess saw the worry on Rick's face. "What's the problem?" she asked him. "We know now that Lendax isn't dangerous."

"Rick knows a little more than that, don't you, Rick?" said Agnew.

Rick nodded, shocked at what Agnew was planning to do. "Keep away from him!" he said to Jess. "Lendax is like any other drug. You have to take it the right way, or it can be very dangerous. If it mixes with your blood too quickly, it could even stop your heart."

As they stepped back from Agnew, Rick looked around the gallery for a weapon. On a near wall, there was a loose metal handle. It was used to operate the main lights above the hall.

Rick wondered if he could reach the handle. He continued to step away from Agnew toward the wall.

"I have to hurry," said the professor. He looked from Rick to Jess with a smile. "After all, I do have a prize to receive. And this is the perfect opportunity to reveal the terrible results of the Lendax trial. By tomorrow, the whole world will think that the drug cannot be trusted."

Agnew stepped closer to Jess. He was holding the syringe in front of him and his voice was rising with excitement. "But first," he said, "you both have a part to play in my story, don't you?"

The professor's meaning was very clear. Rick didn't have time to reach the metal handle. He had to act now! He threw himself forward to push Jess away from Agnew's reach. But as Rick pushed, Agnew, older but still strong and fit, moved forward quickly and pushed the Lendax syringe into Rick's neck. As Rick cried out with the pain from the syringe, he turned and shouted to Jess, "Run!" But Jess stood frozen in terror.

The look of horror in Jess's eyes was the last thing he saw as Rick slowly fell to the floor.

Chapter 12

Catching a killer

"I'm afraid that I have no choice."

"Professor, please . . ."

"I can't let you leave now, can I?"

"I won't tell anyone. I promise."

"There's only one way to be sure of that."

One voice was shaking with fear. The other voice was hard and determined. Slowly, Rick's head cleared. He could feel his heart beating hard against his chest. Sickness was rising to his throat. He wanted only to lie still and to sleep. As his eyes focused again, he saw the back of Agnew's feet. He knew that it was safe to turn his head and look up.

Agnew was turned away from Rick. The professor was stepping toward Jess with a syringe in his hand. She was standing against the wall. Tears were running down her face, and her body was shaking with terror.

"I'm really very sorry," Agnew was saying. "I didn't plan for you both to die. But I promise that you will be the last victim of Doctor Rick Jamieson."

As Agnew moved closer to Jess, Rick slowly rose to his feet. No one saw him. The professor was concentrating on Jess, and his body hid Rick from her view. With an enormous effort, Rick reached for the metal handle. It felt so heavy in his weak hands. As the professor raised the syringe toward Jess's neck, Rick needed all his strength. He swung the metal handle at Agnew and hit him hard on the back of the neck. For a brief moment, the professor seemed to freeze. A look of shock was on his face. And then, slowly, Agnew collapsed on the floor.

Rick was shaking all over. He looked at Jess and tried to smile. As she wiped the tears from her face, she looked amazed. She quickly picked up the syringe that Agnew had dropped. Together, Rick and Jess looked down at the professor. On his knees, Agnew looked so much older.

"How?" whispered Agnew. He was looking up at Rick in surprise. His face was twisted in pain. "I gave you a whole syringe of Lendax. You should be dead."

Rick took his bottle of pills from his pocket. "Beta-blockers, Professor," he said. Jess still looked puzzled. "They're the opposite of Lendax," he explained to her. "Lendax makes the heart beat faster, but beta-blockers help to calm it." Rick shook the bottle of pills. "They saved me."

Agnew shook his head. All his previous confidence had disappeared. "This isn't over," he said. "You've no proof. No one will believe you. I'm a respected doctor."

"They don't have to believe me. The police will find the money that you've invested with Trodan. Then they'll know what I tell them is true."

Agnew smiled. "You told me yourself, Rick, it's not a crime to make money. Everyone in the world is trying to make money. That proves nothing. You need evidence."

A low, angry voice came from the corridor. "Let me worry about the evidence, Professor." It was Detective Anderson. Kramer was standing beside him. Behind them, six policemen were pointing their guns at Agnew. "Now put your hands up," said Anderson.

As the police took Agnew away, Anderson turned to Rick. "There's a police officer outside. He's still shaking after you held that syringe to his neck. Can I suggest an apology? But first you can tell me what this is all about."

Rick still felt faint. Jess helped him to stand as he nodded. "It's about money," he said. "It's always about money. Tamsus is one of two major pharmaceutical companies in the country. The other one is called Trodan. If people thought that Lendax was dangerous, Trodan would benefit. So Agnew invested all his money in Trodan. He then planned to reveal the results of the Lendax trial. And he's a famous doctor. Who would suspect him?"

"He also works for Tamsus," said Jess. "No one would imagine that he would actually want Lendax to fail."

The detective looked puzzled. "But Agnew needed to be sure that everyone would learn about the trial results. How could he guarantee that?"

"Easy," answered Rick. "He was going to announce the results of the trial today at the conference. He was going to tell everyone that people had died while taking Lendax."

"But then Rick got involved," said Jess. "Agnew tried to persuade him to speak to the newspapers instead. If Rick had done that, the professor's name would never have been involved."

"It makes sense," nodded Anderson. "And as a trial doctor, Agnew had access to all the victims. Perhaps he told the patients that they needed to take the extra Lendax as part of the trial."

"Exactly. Elizabeth Wiley was his first victim. After her death, my friend Will Sutton began to suspect that something was wrong. So Agnew killed him. The professor made it look like a climbing accident. Ask Agnew where he was on the morning of Will's death. I bet that he won't have a good answer."

"OK, Doctor," said Anderson, smiling for once. "You're free to go."

Two days later, Rick walked back into the clinic. Under his arm was the local newspaper. There were two main stories. According to the first, the police were questioning Professor Charles Agnew about the murders in the city. In the second, Tamsus was going to make a lot of money from the release of their new drug Lendax.

Rick glanced at the article again and shook his head. "According to the National Institute for Mental Health," it read, "more than 18.8 million American adults have suffered from depression in the last year. Over sixty-five percent of those adults have received treatment." He closed the newspaper, knocked on Kramer's door and walked into the office.

"Come in, Rick!" called Kramer. "I have some very good news. After that business with Agnew, Victor Adams is delighted with you. He has promised to give us a very good price for his drugs. And Trodan called me this morning. They want us to manage a new trial for them. It seems that you're now famous! They asked especially for you. They're offering to pay the clinic and also give you an enormous bonus. This could be the start of a great relationship with Trodan as well!"

Kramer smiled. "Isn't it great? I told them that you'll start work on the trial immediately."

"No," answered Rick. "I'm not going to do any trials, for Trodan or for anyone else."

Kramer sighed and shook his head. "You're angry, Rick. I can see that. I know you think that I was wrong."

"You were wrong, Ian. Our patients come to us for help. And you stopped me from helping them. We might have been able to save some of those Lendax patients. If you had given me the details of the trial, I could have warned them."

"But you must understand why I couldn't do that! We need the pharmaceutical companies on our side. We're a business! And the pharmaceutical companies are our partners in business. I can't afford to upset them. They're vital to us if we want the clinic to survive."

"You're a doctor, Ian," answered Rick, "not a businessman. I became a doctor because I want to help people, not because I want to get rich."

Kramer smiled. "You're an adult, Rick. Surely you can see that everything is business. Everything! Behind everything, there's money. And without money, you have nothing!"

Kramer walked around the desk. He was shouting now. "You think that health is different from everything else in this world, Rick. You think that patients deserve to be treated. But everything has a price. Do I deserve a free holiday because I haven't had one in three years? Do I deserve a free car because I don't already have one? No! And you don't deserve your health because you haven't got it. You have to pay for health like you pay for everything else!"

"Except health isn't a luxury," answered Rick, quietly. "Health isn't just for the rich."

"Rick, this is the real world. You can't help everyone, even if you want to. There is a system. It isn't perfect, but it works. You're a good doctor. If you can learn to work with that system, you'll do well."

Rick shook his head, but Kramer went on. "You could do a lot of good for the clinic and for our patients. And soon, it'll be time for me to retire. When that day comes, I'll need someone to take over the clinic. That could be you."

Rick shook his head again. "I suppose I should thank you for that offer. But I don't want to be involved with your clinic any longer. I enjoy my work. I enjoy helping people. But I don't want to become like you. You think that a patient is nothing more than a business opportunity!"

"Your head is full of dreams, Rick. One day you'll realize that."

"Maybe," Rick smiled. "Meanwhile, you can find yourself another doctor."

Kramer nodded. "If that's what you want."

"Good-bye, Ian," said Rick. He stepped toward the door.

"You had better clear your office before you go."

Rick thought again of the bottle of beta-blockers that he had left in his desk. Then he shook his head. "I don't need anything from my office."

A few seconds later, Rick stepped outside. The sun was shining. It was a perfect spring morning.

"Congratulations!"

Rick turned to see Jess. She was waiting on the sidewalk, with a big smile on her face.

"What do you mean?" he asked.

"I've just spoken to my boss in Paris," Jess said. "He'd be very happy to give you a job. He says that you sound perfect for World United."

"That's very good news. Thank you."

Jess stepped forward and kissed him. "It is good news, isn't it?" she said. "You can buy me lunch to celebrate!"

Together, arm in arm, they set off down the street.

Review: Chapters 1–4

A. Match the characters in the story with their descriptions.

1. Will Sutton
2. Adrian Blake
3. Rick Jamieson
4. Ian Kramer
5. Jessica Blake
6. Detective Anderson
7. Anna Richards
8. Professor Agnew

a. Lendax patient who has jumped out a window
b. the sister of a Lendax victim
c. Lendax victim who lives on Beacon Hill
d. doctor who gives advice to Tamsus
e. doctor who finds the first Lendax victim
f. owner of the psychiatry clinic
g. doctor who dies while climbing
h. Boston police officer

B. Choose the best answer for each question.

1. How does Will Sutton fall when he is climbing?
    a. He jumps.
    b. He slips on the wet rock.
    c. He is pushed.
    d. He loses his balance.

2. Why is Ian Kramer really worried about Will's death?
    a. He will have to tell Will's family.
    b. He will have to find another doctor.
    c. It might affect the conference.
    d. The police will visit him to ask questions.

3. Why does Rick suffer from panic attacks?
   a. He is naturally nervous.
   b. He doesn't drink enough water.
   c. He was in a car accident.
   d. He doesn't like heights.

C. Circle the correct word or phrase in italics to complete each sentence.

1. Rick and Will were *best friends / enemies*.
2. At first, Jess thinks that Rick killed her *boss / brother*.
3. *Ian Kramer / Professor Agnew* will continue with Will's drug trial.
4. Rick takes beta-blockers to help his *panic attacks / driving*.
5. Jess is worried that *Ian Kramer / Lendax* has killed her brother.
6. Ian Kramer is *calm / worried* about the conference.

D. Fill in each blank with the correct answer.

1. Will discovers a terrible secret and decides to tell ______.
2. A company called ______ has agreed to contribute to the cost of the conference.
3. A racing heart, shaking hands, and fast breathing are all signs of ______.
4. ______ hits Rick over the head with a light.
5. Lendax has already been given a(n) ______ to show that it is safe.
6. Rick and Jess meet ______ in a bar.

Review: Chapters 5–8

A. Read each statement and circle whether it is true (T) or false (F).

1. Agnew tells Rick to contact the police. T / F

2. Detective Anderson admires Victor Adams. T / F

3. Rick can be certain that someone has tried to kill him and Jess. T / F

4. Rick is afraid for Jess's safety. T / F

5. Jess is disgusted to learn that Rick takes beta-blockers. T / F

6. Ian Kramer and Rick have a good relationship. T / F

B. Choose the best answer for each question.

1. At the Tamsus office, why does Rick take the stairs instead of the elevator?

a. He wants some exercise.

b. He is afraid of a panic attack in the elevator.

c. Jess tells him to keep out of the elevator.

d. He is chasing Victor Adams's receptionist.

2. How does Victor Adams respond to Rick's concerns about the trial?

a. He leaves to play golf.

b. He gives Rick a list of all the trial patients.

c. He warns Rick to keep quiet.

d. He refuses to stop the trial.

3. Why does Detective Anderson suspect Rick for the murders?

a. Rick has blood on his clothes.

b. Rick has a history of dangerous behavior.

c. Rick is linked to all the patients through the clinic.

d. Detective Anderson doesn't like doctors.

4. Why is Kramer upset with Rick?

a. Rick isn't working hard enough.

b. The pharmaceutical companies might learn that Rick is a murder suspect.

c. Rick is getting too friendly with Jess.

d. Kramer has found out about Rick's beta-blockers.

C. Complete the crossword using the clues below

Across

1. Rick suspects that a man called _______ might have killed Will.
4. Gabriel Moranto's apartment is by the North End _______.
6. Rick and Jess meet Agnew in a _______.
8. The mechanic warns Rick to tell the _______ about the broken jeep.
9. Sebastian _______ is a Lendax patient living in Charlestown.
10. Tamsus has been working on Lendax for _______ years.
11. Rick takes beta-blockers because he doesn't like small _______.
13. Professor Agnew is going to receive a _______ at the conference.
14. Rick suggests that Gabriel Moranto was _______ -handed.

Down

1. World United is based in the city of _______.
2. If the conference goes well, Tamsus has guaranteed the clinic a cheap _______ of their drugs.
3. The _______ has already given Tamsus a license to sell Lendax.
5. When Will died Professor Agnew said he was in _______.
6. Rick's jeep has a problem with the _______.
7. The boss of Tamsus is called Victor _______.
12. When Rick arrived at the Tamsus elevator, he felt the signs of a _______ attack.

Review: Chapters 9–12

A. Fill in each blank with the correct answer.

1. By threatening to harm the policeman, Rick forces Detective Anderson to drop his ______.
2. Rick entered the Conference Center through the ______ doors.
3. Professor Agnew tries to persuade Jess that ______ is the murderer.
4. Lendax doesn't harm Rick because of his ______.
5. Rick uses a metal ______ as a weapon.
6. At the end, Rick decides to take a job with ______.

B. Read each statement and circle whether it is true (T) or false (F).

1. Rick sees Ian Kramer leaving Sebastian Doyle's apartment. T / F
2. Sebastian Doyle has died peacefully in his bed. T / F
3. Rick sees a surprising name on the detective's list. T / F
4. Rick shoots a policeman as he tries to escape. T / F
5. A bus takes Rick to the Conference Center. T / F
6. The Conference Center is empty when Rick arrives. T / F
7. Ian Kramer killed Will Sutton. T / F
8. Rick and his boss become good friends. T / F

C. Choose the best answer for each question.

1. When Rick sees someone leaving Sebastian Doyle's apartment, he doesn't follow. Why not?

a. He is afraid.

b. He is running away from the police.

c. Sebastian Doyle might need urgent help.

d. Rick can't open the elevator door.

2. In the Conference Center, Rick looks down into the crowd. Who does he see?

a. Professor Agnew and Jess

b. Ian Kramer and Victor Adams

c. Detective Anderson and Will Sutton

d. Jess and her brother, Adrian

3. By the end, Victor Adams is delighted with Rick. Why?

a. Rick saved Victor's life.

b. Rick has proved that Lendax is not dangerous.

c. Rick has agreed to work for Tamsus.

d. Rick has agreed to give Lendax to all his patients.

Answer Key

Chapters 1–4

A:

1. g; **2.** c; **3.** e; **4.** f; **5.** b; **6.** h; **7.** a; **8.** d

B:

1. c; **2.** c; **3.** c

C:

1. best friends;
2. brother;
3. Ian Kramer;
4. panic attacks;
5. Lendax;
6. worried

D:

1. the police;
2. Tamsus;
3. a panic attack;
4. Jess;
5. license;
6. Professor Agnew

Chapters 5–8

A:

1. T; **2.** F; **3.** F; **4.** T; **5.** F; **6.** F

B:

1. b; **2.** d; **3.** c; **4.** b

C:

Across

1. Patrick; **4.** Church; **6.** bar; **8.** police; **9.** Doyle; **10.** nine; **11.** spaces; **13.** prize; **14.** right

Down

1. Paris; **2.** supply; **3.** government; **5.** California; **6.** brakes; **7.** Adams; **12.** panic

Chapters 9–12

A:

1. gun; **2.** kitchen; **3.** Rick; **4.** beta-blockers; **5.** handle; **6.** World United

B:

1. F; **2.** F; **3.** T; **4.** F; **5.** F; **6.** F; **7.** F; **8.** F

C:

1. c; **2.** b; **3.** b

Background Reading:

Spotlight on . . . Drugs

Read the passage about drug trials below and on page 104. Then answer the questions below.

Drug trials are organized by health experts in order to test a new drug. They do this by comparing the effects of the new drug to the current treatments available. The number of patients involved in a drug trial varies enormously, from thousands all around the world to only twenty or thirty. Volunteer patients take the drug, and then the results are carefully checked by doctors.

Patient safety is very important. New drugs are often tested on animals before they are tested on humans.

It is sometimes possible to take part in a trial even if you are healthy. But for every drug trial patient, there are both possible benefits and risks.

1. Would you take part in a drug trial if you were healthy?
2. Imagine you are in charge of a drug trial and a patient dies. Would you automatically end the trial?
3. Do you think it is fair to test drugs on animals?

Benefits

- You can play an active part in your own health care.
- It gives you a chance to use new drugs before anyone else can use them.
- You will receive expert medical care during the trial.
- You will be helping others by contributing to medical research.
- You might be paid for your involvement.

Risks

- The new drug might cause unpleasant or serious problems.
- The trial might take a lot of time.
- The new drug might not be effective.

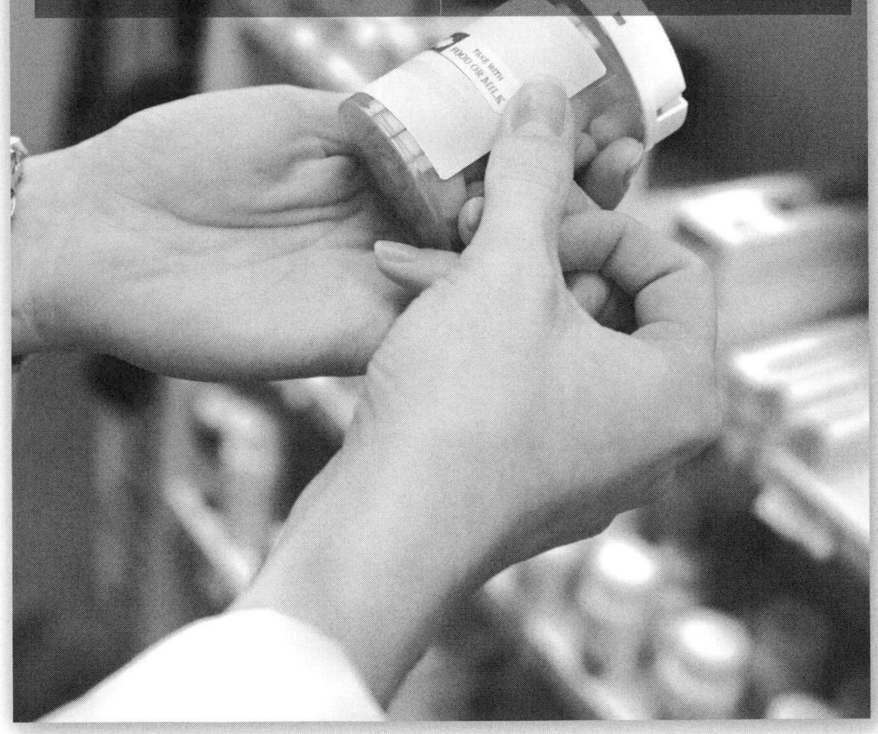

Background Reading:

Spotlight on . . . Depression

Read the passage about depression and answer the questions on the next page.

Depression is an illness that can affect anyone. No one knows exactly what causes it. About two out of three adults suffer from depression at some time in their life, and it is more common in women than in men. Some people worry that it is a sign of weakness, but many great world leaders have had depression, including Winston Churchill.

Possible Signs of Depression

- Sadness and perhaps crying a lot
- Loss of enjoyment
- No interest in eating, or perhaps eating too much
- Problems getting to sleep or waking very early
- Feeling tired all the time
- Loss of interest in sex
- Feeling nervous or easily angered
- Feeling guilty or hopeless
- Having difficulty concentrating
- Thinking of trying to kill yourself
- Headaches, chest pains, or general aches

If you have one or more of these signs for more than two weeks, you should consider seeing a doctor.

Treatment

Most people do recover from depression. If you are suffering from the illness, a doctor might suggest that you

- talk to a friend, relative, or expert about your problems.
- exercise every day.
- try antidepressant medicine.

1. Some people think depression is a sign of weakness. Why do you think this is?
2. Do you think depression is likely to be more common in the modern world? If so, why?
3. Why do you think exercise is often a good treatment for depression?

Background Reading:

Spotlight on . . . The Creation of a New Drug

Read the information about new drug creation and answer the questions on the next page.

It takes many years and hundreds of millions of dollars to create a new drug. Only a very small number of drugs pass all the safety tests and make it to market. It can take as many as twelve years before a new drug can be sold in pharmacies. Despite the time and expense, it is still a very profitable industry.

Developing a New Drug

Early Development

The new drug is tested by scientists. Sometimes it is tested on animals. Many thousands of drugs fail at this stage.

Human Trials

Sometimes as many as sixty separate trials are needed.

Government Approval

The drug can only be sold when the government is confident that the drug is safe.

Checking for Safety

The drug's safety is still tested long after it is released for sale.

The pharmaceutical companies spend a lot of money advertising their drugs. They need to sell enough to pay not only for the new drug itself, but also for all the other drugs that have failed the tests. And they need to do this before other companies can start to copy their new drug.

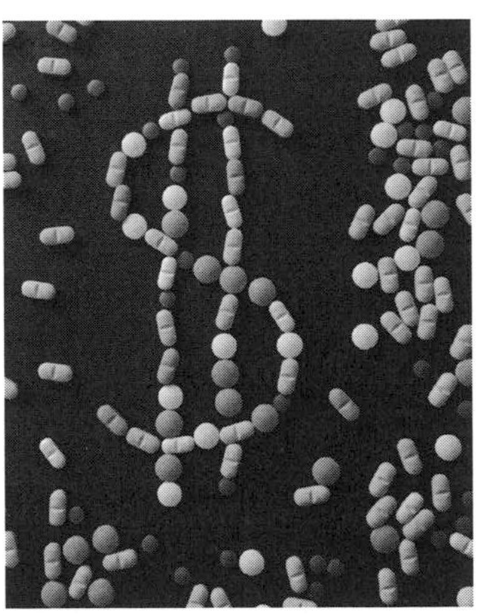

1. Do you think it is right for pharmaceutical companies to profit from ill health?
2. Should the advertising of drugs be limited in any way?
3. Should individuals' access to medicines have anything to do with their personal wealth?

Glossary

antidepressant (*n.*) a kind of drug that acts against depression

beta-blockers (*n.*) drugs used to control high blood pressure, or to treat panic attacks

brake fluid (*n.*) a liquid used in a car's brakes

conference (*n.*) a large professional meeting; a convention

grip (*v.* & *n.*) a firm, strong hold on something

jeep (*n.*) a type of strongly built car made to travel over rough ground

lamp (*n.*) a light

mercy (*n.*) sympathy, compassion

panic (*n.*) a state of uncontrolled fear

pharmaceutical (*n.*) relating to the manufacture of drugs

prescription (*n.*) an order from a doctor for medicines

psychiatry (*n.*) the branch of medicine that deals with mental diseases

(commit) suicide (*v.*) kill oneself

syringe (*n.*) a device doctors use to get blood out of people

NOTES